KINVARA
A SEAPORT TOWN ON GALWAY BAY

KINVARA

A SEAPORT TOWN ON GALWAY BAY

Written by Caoilte Breatnach

Compiled by Anne Korff

Tír Eolas

First published in 1997 by Tír Eolas, Newtownlynch,
Kinvara, Co. Galway.

Text copyright   © Caoilte Breatnach
Historical photographs   © Listed sources
Contemporary photographs   © Anne Korff, except
                            pages 28, 50 Thomas
                            Quinn, pages 67, 114
                            Veronica   Nicholson

Compiled by Anne Korff

British Library Cataloguing in Publication Data.
A catalogue record for this book is available from the
British Library.
ISBN 1-873821-07-7

Tír Eolas acknowledges the generous support of the
Merriman Inn and Restaurant, Kinvara.

Cover and layout: Anne Korff, Johan Hofsteenge
Typesetting: Johan Hofsteenge
Printed in Ireland by Betaprint International Ltd.

PREFACE

A striking feature of the photographs in this book is that they were taken as snapshots of an era. Aspects such as aesthetic quality were not foremost in the photographers' minds; they were more concerned with recording everyday scenes. Consequently, we are presented with an authentic image of rural life, taken, no doubt, by people who valued the importance of presenting an accurate record of life as they knew it.

The pictures in this book are intended as a representative selection of the many photographs taken in and around Kinvara between the 1880s and the 1960s. Where some of them come from, we do not know. We do know that the Kinvara photographers, Tomás Ó hEidhin, Christy Greene and unnamed others were the first to take it upon themselves in the early 1900s to keep a pictorial record of their day.

Tomás Ó hEidhin (1873-1943) was born in the townland of Killina, on the Gort road, and worked as a professional photographer, teacher and water diviner. Christy Greene (1899-1969) was born in Kinvara. He ran Green's pub and grocery with his brother, Sonny, and took photographs as a hobby.

In the 1950s, Robert Cresswell, then a young student of anthropology, compiled a photographic record of life in Kinvara. Based on his research, the Institut d'Ethnologie (Paris) published his book, *Une communauté rurale De l'Irlande*, in 1969. We are indebted to him for having made some of his photographs available to us.

Had it not been for a number of people who, in the 1970s, recognised the value of preserving Kinvara's pictorial heritage, this collection would have been much the poorer. In 1976, Dr Paddy Greene, then living in the USA, visited his native town of Kinvara. He videoed some of the older generation recounting their lives and telling stories and anecdotes of their youth in the 1920s and 1930s. Paddy Greene took it upon himself to borrow as many photographs as he could from local people, and arranged, at his own expense, to have black and white slides made in Dublin.

Around the same time, the Crushua artist, Thomas Quinn, had been doing similar work, also on an entirely voluntary basis, borrowing prints such as Tomás Ó hEidhin's surviving photographs, making new negatives, and building up an archive of local interest, including many of his own photographs. Máirtín Greene had become the proud guardian of his father's work and spent many of his free hours visiting the older generation in a race against time trying to learn about and identify the people depicted on Christy Greene's pictures.

Dr Greene in the meantime had organised a very successful slide show and lecture, published a pamphlet and carried out exhaustive research into historical documents relating to Kinvara. Tom Quinn organised a number of photographic exhibitions held during annual festivals such as Cruinniú na mBád and Fleadh na gCuach.

Others with a keen interest in the parish discussed the prospect of Kinvara Community Council publishing a local magazine on a regular basis, and *Trácht* came into being in the mid-1980s, edited by Jeff O'Connell. This provided a forum for the considerable talents of John Flatley, Toddy Byrne, the late Jimmy O'Connor, Stan Mac Eoin, Jeff O'Connell himself and many others who had an interest in local history and community affairs.

At the same time, Jeff O'Connell and Anne Korff established *Tír Eolas* publishers, producing their first Rambler's Guide & Map of Kinvara, followed by a series of guides and maps of the Burren and South Galway.

With the support of the Community Council, Stan Mac Eoin, who also had been one of those involved in the Doorus folklore group, *Scoil Éigse Dúras*, was foremost with others in encouraging appreciation of the wealth of local folklore, both in Irish and in English. Jeff O'Connell wrote two books about Kinvara's parish history in 1988 (*Kinvara History — A Family Affair* and *St Coleman's Church, Kinvara*) and, fascinated by the intricacies of the historical landscape of his adopted home, plunged like a playful child into the documented history of the parish.

The compilation of photographs published in this book is the result of an arduous selection process undertaken by Anne Korff of *Tír Eolas* publishers. Having been entrusted by Dr Paddy Greene, Tom Quinn and others with about 200 negatives, prints and slides, she set herself the task of selecting a series of images which would reflect the lives of Kinvara's people, as well as the changing social and economic

traditions. It proved difficult, however, to portray people's daily activities, as it was uncommon, prior to the 1940s, to photograph people at work.

In 1995, Anne Korff photographed buildings and streets in the town. These photos are set in contrast to the earlier ones depicting the same views, thus reflecting the town's changing architectural fabric. The fact that Anne is a newcomer to Kinvara may have been an advantage in her approach, allowing her to make a representative selection relevant to both the local and the general viewer.

All notes and reference material made available to *Tír Eolas*, were then handed to Caoilte Breatnach, who was asked to write the text accompanying the photographs.

Historical and contemporary sources, though often sketchy, are sometimes astoundingly detailed. To these documented records a local flavour has been added — mainly based on older people from the district who viewed the photographs and who, in most instances, could remember things which in just two generations have become almost forgotten. Without the availability of information such as this, the task of writing the text would have been impossible.

The old people believed that, when a person died, his or her photograph would begin to fade. Whatever the truth about that, memory, in any event, does fade. Precise details become sketchy and, with the passing of time, people forget some of the things they took for granted and paid no heed to in the past. Such details take on a new meaning in future years, providing an important link with our understanding of the past.

One of the most frequent comments one hears today, when seeking information about the recent past from the older generation, is that you are 20 years too late. One becomes acutely aware that every passing year sees the demise of some great local character, a man or woman, whose life and memory spanned an era which, no doubt, will become a subject of study for future generations. Another frequent remark was echoed by a woman who lamented: " Oh, if only my father were here now, he'd remember it all. We should have talked more to the older people and written it down. We never did..."

What brought these photographs to life was listening to the local people who viewed them and gave willingly of their time. Their rich descriptions of past events could fill many more pages beyond the scope of this book. Like photographs, they constitute snippets of time and place, heard and experienced by a generation gifted with a power of memory and a rich means of expression rare today.

We are indebted to everyone listed below for their help. Others asked not to be mentioned, and we extend our sincere thanks to them as well. Everyone we approached was most helpful and forthcoming with information, including the eight people who also read the draft. Likewise, thanks to all who helped identify the people in the photographs, a job which sometimes led us to new sources. If identification remained in doubt, we left out the suggested name. Every effort has been made for accuracy, with doubtful information being double checked. Any error brought to our attention will be corrected in due course.

Táimid thar a bheith buíoch do 'chuile dhuine a thug cúnamh is a bhí sásta páirt a ghlacadh sa bhfiontar seo. Nár leaga Dia sibh is go maire sibh an céad!

We gratefully acknowledge the facilities made available by Galway County Libraries and the Irish Folklore Dept (Roinn Bhéaloideas Éireann).

For their hospitality and their assistance, and for pointing us in the right direction, many thanks in particular to the following:

Eibhlín Bn Uí Chuaig and Pat McCooke; Anne and Jimmy Conole; Ger, May and Val Conneely; Tom Leech; the Connolly family of *Tigh Uí Chonghaile*; Máirín Doddy; Alan Clarke; the Linnane family (Ballycleara); the Tully family (Kinvara); Paddy Connolly; Paddy Joe Connolly; Kathleen Kenny; Ann Niland; Mary Maloney and Mick Connolly (Gortaboy); Tony Divinney; Michael Loughrey; Nonie Connolly; Micky and Patricia Martin (Dunguaire); Martin Greene; Paddy Geraghty; Finola Murphy; John and Denise Griffin; Colie Winkle; Maura Mongan; Martin and Maura Fallon; Paddy O'Loughlin, Mary Murray/Green; Páraic Kilkelly; John and Frank Flatley; Tommy St George; Gerry and Teresa Sweeney (Kinvara); John and Mathilda Leech; Marie Winkle; Stan Mac Eoin; Gerry Ryan; Tommy Corless; Jeff O'Connell; Thomas Quinn; Dr Paddy Greene; Robert Cresswell; Carmel O'Donoghue; John Flanagan; Séadna Tóibín; Petra Bhreatnach; Deasún Breatnach, Máirtín Ó Briain; Dáithí Ó Cróinín; Annette Möker; Veronica Nicholson.

Caoilte Breatnach and Anne Korff

INTRODUCTION

The first record of Kinvara as a market place dates to 21 February, 1615, when Oliver Martyn, an Anglo-Norman then resident at Dunguaire Castle, was granted a licence to hold a Saturday market in the parish of *Kiloveragh*, as it was known then in English. Kiloveragh could be an anglicization of *Coill Uí Fhiachrach*, which was translated in 1839 by the antiquarian, Dr O'Donovan, as *Wood of the O'Hynes*.

Dunguaire Castle, built around 1510, had been the principal seat of the Uí Fiachra Aidhne clan (the O'Hynes), but was no longer their property at this stage, having transferred to the Earl of Clanrickard, and been leased to Oliver Martyn. The charter granted to Martyn was the precursor of the tolls and customs in Kinvara. These levies were payable respectively on fair days and upon arrival of cargo boats at the quay. Customs duties were abolished when Kinvara harbour ceased to be a private dock in the early 1900s, though tolls continued to be levied on market days up to the late 1950s.

We are told that in 1599, Red Hugh O'Donnell, the famous Donegal chieftain, raided Connaught. His main target, apart from the Earl of Clanrickard, was the Earl of Thomond, who refused to aid the northern alliance against the Crown. Subsequently, he rested his army at Dunguaire Castle. The days of such daring escapades would soon be numbered, however, as would the tenure of those who dared shelter the likes of O'Donnell.

Two years later saw O'Donnell march south again, only to witness the decimation of the Irish armies at Kinsale, a battle which changed the course of Irish history. The dispossession of the influential O'Heyne chieftains was now just a matter of time. According to an inquisition in 1608, the lands of the O'Heyne clan comprised some 8,640 acres. By 1636, their influence had declined considerably, and much of their lands passed into the hands of the fourth Earl of Clanrickard, Richard De Burgo, Lord President of Connaught and Governor of Galway. De Burgo, incidentally, had played a strategic role in the Battle of Kinsale.

The lands of Kinvara, or *Cinn Mhara* in Irish, were to be confiscated in 1641 in accordance with the Act of Survey and Distribution. In 1642, we read of one Richard Martyn, Mayor of Galway, residing at Dunguaire Castle (*Dún Guaire*, the fort of King Guaire). And around 1920, so the story goes, his descendant, Edward Martyn, gave the castle to his friend, the novelist and co-founder of the Abbey Theatre, Oliver St John Gogarty, for a bottle of champagne. Gogarty planned to renovate the castle but never did.

During the 1600s, access to Kinvara by sea would have been much less cumbersome than by road or even by dirt track. In terms of infrastructural development, almost all of Ireland lagged far behind England and the Continent. Given the imposing castle at Dunguaire and St Coman's church nearby, Kinvara might well have been more advanced than other settlements of the day. The establishment of towns and villages was actually a very late occurrence in Ireland. Apart from Dublin, a relatively small town at the time, the only other major Irish towns of importance in terms of affluence and trade were Waterford, Drogheda and Galway.

Compared with the European Continent, exports were rudimentary in the extreme. The country's key exports were mainly fish and hides, there being no live export of cattle. Wool was a predominantly export-oriented business in the hands of the Normans in the south-east of Ireland. The Normans were granted the entire province of Connaught in 1177 and, by the 1600s, had long since established themselves in the province, becoming culturally integrated to a degree and forming ties of mutual interest with the Irish chieftains of the day. There were trading links, too, between France, Spain and Galway, and possibly even Kinvara. Charles Ffrench Blake Forster, in *The Irish Chieftains* or *A Struggle for the Crown*, published in 1872, refers to a French masted ship anchored off Crushua, Kinvara Bay, in the late 1600s.

Fear of a Spanish invasion was the driving force behind the English conquest of Ireland in the late 1500s. Resistance was crushed, and thousands transported to the Indies and the Caribbean for the slave trade, many of whom are believed to have sailed from Galway. After the decisive Battle of Kinsale in 1601, Ireland became effectively subservient to the rule of England, whose colonial status was to be fully consolidated by Oliver Cromwell's forces in the 1650s.

The change of property ownership must have been phenomenal. Parliament officials such as the Earl of Mountrath, Sir Charles Coote, Colonel Carey Dillon and Henry Waddington, all acquired lands in the Kinvara area. As was customary in all wars, those funding the Irish campaigns and enforcing English rule were awarded large tracts of land. This factor, together with the increasing demand abroad for live cattle and timber, saw the Irish woodlands being cleared on a massive scale.

The growth of an export-oriented economy, chiefly exploited by adventurers who were unaffected by the conservation controls governing England and the Continent, resulted in the rapid decline of vast forests of sessile oak, ash and, to a lesser extent, pine and yew. In 1600, about 35% of the countryside was covered in forests. By 1700, the percentage of broad-leaved trees remaining in Ireland was under 2 per cent, a meagre figure that would begin to be surpassed only in 1994. Apart from the enormous quantities of timber reputedly exported to England and Holland for the shipbuilding industry, considerable quantities of oak were split into barrel-staves in the now burgeoning cooperage trade. Much wood was consumed also in foundries in the manufacture of bar iron and artillery. In a land denuded of tree-cover, packs of wolves now ravaged the cleared countryside and eventually became extinct in Ireland.

In 1611, an attempt to legislate for the preservation of Irish woodlands failed in the Westminster Parliament, and entrepreneurs were granted charters to export timber for another 21 years. The woodlands in the territory of the Aidhne Clan also had provided cover for guerilla warfare by those of the O'Heynes still hoping against hope to regain their lands. Apart from the few remaining O'Henes and O'Hines recorded in a property record of 1641, one can assume that by this time the remainder was scattered and exiled. In 1709, we find evidence of one Domingo O'Hyne, a young descendant of the O'Hyne-Shaughnessy sept from Caherillaun Castle, being knighted in Madrid. Interestingly, his baptismal sponsors in 1683 were Oliver Martyn of Doorus peninsula and Cristina French of Cahercon townland.

With the population explosion of the 1770s came the increasing demand for agricultural land and the consequent obliteration of the smaller woods of holly, hazel and thorn, which proliferated in the Burren area at the time. The substantial increase in population meant that the *nouveau riche* adventurers and the Anglo-Irish gentry now had large numbers of tenants on whom they could call to build their estates and parklands, which were becoming fashionable in Ireland at the time.

Parklands were planted for the first time with trees such as beech, hitherto unknown in Ireland and much in evidence as majestic, stately trees in estates such as Coole Park, Gort, and Tulira Castle, near Ardrhahan, though less apparent today in the Kinvara demesnes. In terms of domestic architecture, Ireland lingered about a century behind most of Western Europe, with the gentry still living in cramped tower houses or in long, one-storey thatched houses. Given the political unrest and other factors, fortified tower houses were still being extended in the early 1700s by the Frenchs of

Monivea, Co Galway, while others preferred to build large houses on their demesnes, often within sight of the former castle. For the tenants, long-accustomed to living in one-roomed cabins without a chimney, the addition of a chimney to the gable walls of their modest dwellings, and later, in the 1800s, an extra room or two, was a welcome improvement.

With the growth of commerce came the need for more markets and fairs. Towns and villages were built, while fields became shaped by ditch and hedge. The expansion of trade was to result in the transformation of Kinvara. What might have been originally a small settlement around Dunguaire Castle and a scattering of dwellings both in Kinvara itself and in nearby townland of Ballbrannigan — reputedly the site of another castle — now would gradually develop into a port of some significance. With the rapidly growing economy came the realisation of Kinvara's great economic potential, and the more astute merchants of the day seized upon the opportunity and began to develop the district.

One such man was James French, descendant of Robuck French, a Galway merchant who had been 'transplanted' in 1656 by Cromwell to Kileenavara in the parish of Ballindereen, following the Parliamentarian War. Having backed the loser in the civil war in England (Parliament v. Crown), French's property in Galway was confiscated, whereas the O'Heyne chieftains for the most part were dispossessed. Robuck French later was granted or acquired extensive lands in the Kinvara area and on the Doorus peninsula.

His descendant, James French, an improving landlord whose fine residence once stood on the 'Prospect' in Doorus Demesne, built the first pier in Kinvara in 1773, over a naturally occurring breakwater of rocks. The De Basterots, inheritors through marriage of a portion of the large French estate, built their first 'Big House', *Doorus House*, in Parkmore, and made further infrastructural improvements in Kinvara and Doorus. Projects undertaken by the De Basterots included the building of tidal mills in the early 1800s, and at least one windmill. They constructed the causeway at Bridge Lough, connecting the island of Doorus to the mainland, and the raising of the causeway linking Doorus to Aughinish is also attributed to them.

The Penal Laws were meant to diminish the power of the Catholic Church and to disempower the Catholic gentry but are said not to have been very effective in Kinvara. This was due to the greater influence locally of landlords such as the Frenchs who had originally been Catholics, prior to conforming to the Established Protestant Church in order to retain their lands. However, Mass had to be celebrated secretly and priests had a bounty of £5 on their heads.

A contemporary of James French was William Delamain, a Huguenot whose ancestors fled France in the late 1600s. William Delamain was born in Dublin and later settled in Kinvara, firmly ensconcing himself by marrying the daughter of a neighbouring chieftain, Hannagh O'Shaughnessey. He developed lucrative business links with France, and the 'Captain', as he was called, is said to have prospered along with others from the illegal export of wool during the Napoleonic War. Large quantities of brandy and wines, tobacco and teas were exchanged in the smuggling operation. An interesting news item in *The Connaught Journal* of 1 March 1792 reports the seizure of contraband by the Revenue in the village of Nogra, Doorus:

Last Tuesday Messrs. Morrison and Mason, assisted by a party of the 17th Regiment of Foot, seized twenty-three bales of leaf tobacco at a village called Knoggery *(Cnagaire)*, and lodged the same in his Majesty's stores.

The Delamains and their retinue had their own mooring close to Kinvara pier, and are accredited with having built a chapel nearby in 1782. The marriage of Captain William Delamain's son, James, to a cognac merchant's daughter in Jarnac, France, heralded the son's departure in 1760, and their residence, Delamaine Lodge, eventually was sold some 30 years later.

The potato, introduced about 150 years earlier and by then part of the Irish diet, was something James Delamain missed in his adopted home. In April 1768, he thanked the captain of a merchant ship for the offer of potatoes and returned the compliment with some old brandy.

Irish merchants living in the south-west of France at the time always welcomed small consignments of potatoes from Ireland, which arrived as gifts with colleagues travelling on business. A barrel of potatoes would have been as much valued by these

Illustration by Anne Korff

Kinvara as it might have looked in the late 1700s.

1. First quay, c. 50 yards long built by James French in 1773.
2. Delamaine Lodge built by William Delamain, a Huguenot merchant of French descent c. 1760.
3. The Claddagh. Occupants depended mainly on fishing and seaweed gathering for their living.
4. Remains of castle used as coastguard station.
5. Huguenot or 'French chapel', built in 1782.
6. Smythy.
7. Fairgreen.
8. Boat-builder's yard.
9. St Coman's church and graveyard.
10. Market square.
11. Possible residence of Dr. Nicholas Archdeacon, priest in Kinvara from 1798 to 1800.
12. Pound.
13. Windmill.

expatriates as barrels of Irish cheese, hung beef or tongue. Though common in the diet of the upper classes in Ireland, the potato was not being cultivated in France to any great degree, and James Delamain, now partner in Ranson & Delamain in Jarnac, is accredited with having been the first man to plant potatoes in the Cognac region.

In the early 1800s the fast-expanding village of Kinvara came into the possession of Richard Gregory of the Coole estate and he proceeded to make improvements to the harbour, enlarging the pier and adding a dock in 1807. However, the ancient church of St Coman beside the quay, with its surrounding cemetery, stood in the way of Gregory's plans for the town. It must have been with some trepidation that he gave the unorthodox order to clear a section of it for development.

Business by now was booming, with reports of a growing number of fairs and markets in the town. More houses were being built, and lands reclaimed for farming. The harbour was in full use, with upwards of 60 boats sometimes arriving at high tide. Lewis reported in his topographical dictionary in 1837 that two great sheep fairs were held in the town in May and October. Vast quantities of corn were produced, he wrote, not to mention the seaweed landed each spring, valued at £20,000.

However, both the drastic fall in agricultural prices after the Napoleonic wars and the poor harvests in 1817 and 1822 were to have a devastating effect on the growing numbers of destitute tenants. Landlords no longer could collect rents, and middlemen sub-letting meagre plots of land saw much of the land being depleted by a tenantry that had become almost totally dependent on the potato to feed their families.

Unaware or forced to ignore the practice of good husbandry, potatoes continued to be sown year after year in the same ground. Tufts of sparse grassland were dug up and stacked to dry, then burnt and the ashes used as fertiliser. The benefits of illegal acts such as lea-burning (dó bhéiteáil) were shortlived and led to further impoverishment of the land, which took the 'power' out of it, as one man commented in folklore. Then came the Great Famine in the mid-1840s.

It is not easy to visualise the population boom in the Kinvara of that time and the catastrophe that was to follow. Small villages sprung up, flourished and died. Deserted clusters of houses would later become known as famine villages. Others were cleared without trace and converted to grassland. In 1792, the Connaught Journal reported that the population of Kinvara parish had grown to 2,000. Between 1821 and 1831 the number of houses in Kinvara town rose from 64 to 140.

Both Samuel Lewis and Dr John O'Donovan referred to the growing prosperity of the town. By 1841 the population of Kinvara and Doorus had grown to 6,586. Ten years later it had fallen to 4,268 and, by the end of the century, disease, poverty, land-clearance, and emigration drastically reduced the population further. In 1901, of the 106 dwellings in the town, only 86 now were inhabited.

The Great Famine (An Gorta Mór) has been described in some detail in a number of publications by Kinvara Community Council, and is too complex to summarise fully here. Looking back on the Famine 150 years later, one is struck by the physical scars left on the Burren landscape, lonesome clusters of tiny ruins covered in ivy and bramble; nameless headstones scattered and forgotten. Likewise, the Burren's euphemistically termed 'Green Roads', (*Famine roads*, in Irish), wasted famine relief projects, remote and desolate, and slowly being reclaimed by hazel and hawthorn. Momentarily, one catches a glimpse of pale, starving parents together with their children breaking already broken stones in needless public works schemes such as these. Also, the consequent psychological trauma and the dent on a nation's sense of security, self-confidence, and pride in its cultural heritage. People died in their hundreds of disease and starvation, though corn was being exported under armed guard. Complacency and bureaucracy led to countless and unnecessary suffering. Lands were cleared of dwellings to make way for cattle and sheep. Yet despite all this inhumanity, despite the initial refusal of a government far removed from the unfolding tragedy to accept the extent of the calamity, on a local level the situation was quite different.

During the Famine, some landlords in the area did not enforce the collection of rents, most notably the De Basterots and the Gregorys. Moved by the distress of their tenantry, landlords became active on relief committees which, by 1847, were issuing on average 5,400 rations a day in Kinvara (oatmeal, wheatmeal and Indian meal).

Dr Denis J. Hynes, a founder and one time President of the Irish Medical Association. Dr Hynes was much respected in the Kinvara district for his Trojan work during the Famine years. He died at his residence, Seamount House, in 1875 and was succeeded by his son-in-law, Dr William Nally, of Thornville Lodge.

Photographer unknown

By this time the mortality rate in the Galway county workhouses was reaching 25,000 persons per week and, in Kinvara, Dr Denis J. Hynes, another tireless worker who himself fell seriously ill in 1848 but who recovered, had more than his hands full with the dysentery, relapsing fever and typhus, to which two of his own sons succumbed in the 1860s.

A dispensary was opened in Kinvara village and the temporary fever hospital at Foy's Hill, open from 1848-1849, coped as best it could. Below the beautifully situated fever hospital, hundreds of coffin-less burials took place in a mass pit, the hollow of which is still visible today. The local clergy, too, were stretched to the limit. Overcome by grief and exhaustion, the parish priest, Father Patrick Forde, collapsed and died of famine fever in 1846.

By the early 1850s the worst appeared to be over and a degree of optimism began to return. Sir William Gregory's rent books refer to two annual cattle fairs and the likelihood of additional fairs "to meet the rising prosperity of the town." The harbour in Kinvara was a good one, the report stated, and

> is capable of receiving ships of good size and this being a port of Gort, and of very extensive and rich agricultural districts, the trade, at present considerable, must of necessity increase.

However it would take almost another 50 years for Kinvara to recover from the worst effects of the Famine. Those of the compassionate gentry who helped develop Kinvara into a town with great potential, now faced bankruptcy owing to huge debts accrued during the famine years.

James De Basterot found himself in great difficulties with his creditors. Much of De Basterot's estate had already been sold some 50 years earlier to the Lynchs of Renmore, Galway. William Gregory, forced by the Encumbered Estates Court in 1857 to dispose of his assets in Kinvara town and elsewhere watched as his successor, Henry Comerford, and others doubled and trebled existing rents. Evictions were commonplace; simple cabins better known as *bothâin*, were tumbled; tilled ground was turned to pasture for cattle. Father Francis Arthur, the new parish priest, remarked:

> The change of landlords for the greatest portion in this place has rendered this one of the most wretched and deplorable parishes in Ireland.

Following the abortive Young Irelanders' Rising in 1848, Father Arthur, together with his curate, Rev Martin Kelly, sheltered the Young Ireland leader, John Blake Dillon, who was to be tried under the Treason Felony Act. Disguised as a priest, the young rebel was safely conducted to Inishmaan (Aran Islands) by John Holland, a local boatman from Kinvara, whence he sailed for America.

Many people emigrated from Kinvara and Doorus around this time, but no comprehensive figures are available. One of the ships carrying passengers from the Kinvara parish was the *Robert Alexander*, which sailed from Galway to New York in 1849. Others from the parish left in the *Franklin* and the *Henderson* around the same time.

In 1852, the year Doorus national school was opened, Father Arthur staunchly opposed the proselytisers arriving in Kinvara on a *Protestant*

Photographer unknown
Courtesy of Paddy Geraghty

crusade from North Connemara. The abandonment eight years earlier by a Kinvara-born priest of his Catholic religion also aroused much sectarian bitterness at the time. William Burke, or *Jumper Burke*, as he was called, publicly renounced the Church of Rome at Sunday service in St John's (Protestant) Church, Kinvara, and afterwards had to be shielded by the constabulary when stoned by a large crowd. The Protestant chapel and schoolhouse had been located behind the current site of the Merriman Inn. Adding fuel to the bitterness was the fact that Catholics were obliged, following the Tithe Composition Act in 1823, to pay for the upkeep of the local Protestant church and its Minister.

Likewise, the Poor Law Act saw much opposition by householders in the Kinvara and Doorus areas to the collection of exorbitant rates. By the time Reverend Arthur was transferred to Craughwell in 1867, the population of his parish had fallen, in two decades, from 1,800 to 700 families (about 5,500 people).

Kinvara National School, the earliest school built under the National School Act, opened its doors in 1838, near Colman's Church. Other schools soon would be established throughout the parish, replacing the elementary but distinguished *hedge* schools in the townland of Cahernamadra, the Claddagh and Loughcurra townland. Under the new Act, Children whose mother-tongue was Irish were discouraged from speaking their national language and even punished at school for such. Parents were persuaded to acquiesce in a programme designed to prepare a new generation of children for the 'modern' world where Irish had no place.

The great national issues of the day continued to determine the course in which the country was heading. Statesmen campaigning for an Irish parliament were learning the art of political manoeuvring in Westminster. One of these campaigners was Charles Stewart Parnell who, together with his Irish Nationalist Party, aligned himself with the great land agitation organised by the Land League. In 1886, the year Gladstone introduced the Home Rule Bill in Parliament, Parnell passed through Kinvara, where he is said to have addressed a large crowd from the top window of Greene's Hotel.

Charles Stewart Parnell, together with Dr William Nally and one Ms Flatley. Location: either Seamount House or Thornville Lodge. The 1886 by-election in Galway is believed to have brought Parnell to Kinvara.

Whatever political upheavals were affecting the country, trade was booming again in Kinvara, and the port began to thrive once more. Timber and pine staves came from the townland of Derrybrien and the Coole estate, to be shipped out in vessels such as the *Elma* and used as pit-props in Welsh mines. The *Harvest King* (later the *Moby Dick*) is also said to have sailed from Kinvara with timber from Raheen woods, near Kiltartan, Gort. Schooners and hookers appeared frequently on the horizon. Boats were being built near the shore at the *Cnocán*, next to the reputed site of a castle, as shown in the reconstruction drawn on page 13. The Keanes and Patsey Brannelly built great hookers such as the *Lord*, and *An Tonaí* here. Another account tells of *An Tonaí* being built by Brannely in Ballinacourty, Maree in 1892. A saw-pit operated on the quay and blacksmiths were much in demand. Barley was grown in abundance, given the favourable soil conditions in the area. By the early 1900s the total businesses in the town of Kinvara numbered 43, including 23 grocery outlets, 14 pubs, 5 hotels, 4 butchers' stalls, 3 bakeries, 3 forges, 2 tailors' shops, 4 carpentry shops, 1 cobbler, and 2 undertakers.

With the dawning of a new century came a new sense of national pride. Tomás Ó hEidhin, the photographer whose father had once been fined for displaying his name in Irish on a horse cart, became active with others in the newly founded Gaelic League, organising Irish classes and collecting folklore in the area.

Personalities such as Lady Gregory and W.B. Yeats met with Edward Martyn and Oliver St John Gogarty in Doorus House, Parkmore, to discuss the foundation of a national theatre. Across the sea, the poet Francis Fahy continued to write poems and ballads which were to become famous. Paradoxically, the birth of a new state was about to commence and it is at this point that this photographic record begins.

Caoilte Breatnach

O! 'tis sad in Dooras when the tide is low
And the green fields buried 'neath the frost and snow,
And the dark nights dreary with the curlew's cry,
And I thinking, thinking of the days gone by.

O! the happy Summers of the olden days,
And the brown boats sailing through the golden haze,
And the cuckoo calling from the woods within,
And my love beside me and the tide full in.

(From The Tide Full In by Francis Fahy; 1854-1935)

Dedicated to the memory of
Tomás Ó hEidhin, Christy Greene,
and the unknown photographers.

Main Street, 1995

WALKING UP MAIN STREET 1890s

Contrasting starkly with the merchants' formal, slated buildings, the older thatched houses on both sides of the road give a reasonable indication of what the village of Kinvara must have looked like at the beginning of the 1800s.

The woman in the large cloak (right) is standing outside O'Donoghues Pub, later known as Cusack's, prior to Tully's. Further down, a trap and cart await repair outside Paddy Connolly's forge and carpentry workshop.

Johnston's (left) was a spirit merchant, general draper, grocer and ironmonger. Dominic Connolly's thatched shop next door stocked, among other things, rounds of tobacco. Children sent by their fathers for an ounce or two of pipe tobacco watched curiously as the shopkeeper with his curved knife cut the required amount of plug tobacco. If he was short, he'd cut another piece and stick a pin in it to bring it up to the standard weight.

Down the road, a woman enters Coleman's shop, renowned bakers who also made their own candy sticks.

Kinvara's potential as an up-and-coming trading port had been appreciated by the main landlords — Frenchs in the 18th century, De Basterots and Gregorys in the 19th — who made infrastructural improvements in Kinvara and Doorus.

The Great Famine (1845-49) intervened, however, and the town's fortunes declined. The 1851 census recorded a population of 1,102 living in the town. By 1901 it had fallen to 340.

The child in the white smock, standing outside Johnston's, would have no direct memory of the Great Famine. Like all holocausts, generations must pass before the subject may be broached without shame. On the other hand, both men in the picture would have been young lads when, 50 years earlier, hunger, disease and deprivation stalked the land with devastating consequences. Having survived that, they would now witness their own sons and daughters opting for the emigration boat, in search of a better life across the Atlantic.

Photographer unknown
Courtesy of Thomas Quinn

Photographer: Tomás Ó hEidhin

PORTRAIT OF OLD AGE c. 1905

In many of the old photographs by Tomás O hEidhin, portraits were taken against a backdrop of a stone wall covered in ivy, and, as was customary, it is the man who is seated.

Elderly couples like the Donoghues, might well have been less constrained by the fashions of the day than their children, judging from the Victorian style of the dress and the upturned collar of the man. The long dress with the fine embroidered bodice and sleeves is worn over a cotton blouse comprising both collar and cuffs of lace. Her husband's heavy coat or *cóta mór* of wool is worn over a striped suit.

Johnny Donoghue was described as a "small little maneen", and a great one for horses. Farmers brought their mares to his farm near Boston, Tubber, where he kept a stallion.

When visiting her relatives in Loughcurra townland, Annie Donoghue (née Leech) and her husband came by pony and trap. Also described as a great woman for horses, she would accentuate her departure with a touch of drama at the gate, drawing on the reins to get the horse to stand on its hind legs.

Photographer: Tomás Ó hEidhin

THRESHING CORN early 1900s

The corn has been reaped, stooked, stacked and now is being threshed, to separate the grain from the husks and straw. The horse-driven mechanism, visible on the right, operates a long spindle which in turn rotates a drum situated by the group of people on the left. Three horses go round and round (right), each time overstepping the spindle as they go, and the grain-laden sheaves are fed into the rotating drum.

For logistical reasons, this system continued to be used on Island Eddy long after the invention of the cumbersome steam thresher, which contractors hauled from farm to farm once harvesting had been completed.

The mechanisation of farming was to take much of the back-breaking work out of farming. Ironically, though, both social and economic factors eventually led to large reductions in the numbers willing or able to take up farming.

Smallholders in particular would have been well-accustomed to cutting hay with a scythe. The older generation — men and women — were used to harvesting barley and oats with a reaping hook, or sickle, better known to them as a *corrán*. Migrant workers, or spalpeens *(spailpíní)*, were also employed at times like this, moving from farm to farm, county to county.

Neighbours helped each other out too, and the large group or *meitheal* photographed represents a number of families that have joined forces for the threshing operation.

The threshing has probably finished for the day, as there is no sign of the drum. There is time for relaxation, and some tomfoolery. A proud man poses arm in arm beside his beloved (left), whereas the image of the two men in front of the haystack, pretending to point rifles at the camera, gives an indication of the troubled times that are brewing, if not already there.

NORTHAMPTON SCHOOL c. 1902

Northampton national school was opened on 10 May 1853, at a time when Kinvara's population had fallen drastically in the wake of the Famine. The Northampton landlord, James Mahon, died in 1867, and the new proprietor, James Murray, became patron of the school. In 1866, a young Francis Fahy, poet and playwright, was appointed monitor here, a position also held by Annie Leech, shown in the black dress (centre) next to Annie O'Donnell, the 22-year-old teacher.

In the mid 1800s, the national illiteracy rate stood at about 50%. Schooling in Ireland was to have a significant impact, especially in the case of girls, whose rate of literacy had risen from 27% in 1841 to 95% in 1901, compared with 93% for boys, who had a higher level of literacy in 1841 (47%).

Attendance at school in Kinvara was higher in summer than in winter, subject to social conditions and the home environment. Girls especially were kept at home often to help with the general house and farm work or when someone was ill. Likewise, boys' help on the farm was indispensable at certain times of the year, which accordingly would lead to their absence from school.

If the road was the longest route to school, children such as those from the townland of Gortaboy preferred to take the short cut over the fields. Getting a biscuit from Mrs Donnelan on their journey home was a big treat and if a girl had a bit of a chesty cold, the teacher would fold a few newspaper sheets, heat them on the stove, and place them inside her vest.

Some, at least, of the girls in this beautiful photograph would still have found the wearing of boots uncomfortable, much preferring to walk barefoot at home. As to the pinafores worn by the children, one gentleman was reminded of his devilish youth, when, in an act of audacity, he spilt ink over a girl's spotless dress: "I once threw a bottle of ink on her lovely white dress. I was sitting behind her. Many years later I met her and I said: Do you remember the day I threw the ink on your nice dress? I do she says, and do you remember the colour it was? I do, says I to her, it was blue...!"

Cruinniú na mBád festival 1996.

KINVARA QUAY c. 1902

At the turn of the century, Kinvara was a thriving port, serving the entire surrounding countryside. Kinvara quay (45 mtrs) was erected by James French in 1773. Dressed stones from a castle in the townland of Ballybrannigan, believed to be one of the local castles which collapsed during the Lisbon earthquake 18 years earlier, are said to have been employed in the construction of the quay and in house building. Other theories suggest that the ruins of this castle actually stood on, or near the quay itself, as did a coastguard station.

In 1807-8, Richard Gregory of the Coole estate made additional improvements, extending and widening the pier, and adding a dock. A further government granted quay extension opposite Perrse's grain store was completed in 1908.

A man performs a task on the lighter (right), which unburdened schooners in the bay of part of their cargoes. The engine-less lighter, a decommissioned ship, would be towed out to rendezvous with merchant vessels in the bay to lighten their load. This was essential in shallow ports, as schooners such as the *Windermere* (p 33), standing fully-laden in dry dock, would burst their hulls.

The *Fág a' Bealach* next to the lighter was one of the biggest hookers ever built, and belonged to the McDonaghs. In excess of 60 creels line the dock, as hookers unload their cargoes, and on a day like this, upwards of 160 people might be working on the quay.

On the left, hookers lie heeled against the shore: the quay wall had not been built at this stage. A man standing in an ass cart stacks turf being thrown up to him from a boat.

Smoke rising from another hooker (2nd left) signifies cooking below deck. The *bádóirí* (boatmen) also slept in their boats.

At the back (left) is Flatley's yard, where coal was stored, and the number of warehouses lining the quay are testimony to a busy localised industry.

Kinvara-owned hookers are shown, including the 12 metre long *Mary Ann of Galway*, owned by Ned Holland, and built by the Caseys in Maoinis, Connemara, around 1885. Another boat on the right, with the white strip, was built by the Raineys, renowned boat-builders who were based on Tawin peninsula and in Galway.

It is chiefly due to Kinvara's maritime history that the annual *Cruinniú na mBád* festival was established in 1979, to commemorate the trading and social links with Connemara.

Photographer unknown
Courtesy of Tommy Corless

LOADING BARLEY ON THE QUAY c. 1904

Almost 30 people are congregated on the pier head as barley is weighed and unloaded onto a vessel bound for Galway.

Thomas O'Shaughnessey (wearing sou'wester) tips one of the hundreds of bags to be unloaded that day into the boat's hold. Mikey Traynor (left) — a great hurler in his day — stands attentively alongside his brother, Jack, ready to haul the next 2 cwt bag (100 kilos) onto the weighing scale. John Burke surveys the scene from above the cart.

The largest ship exporting barley from Kinvara was the *S.S. Mungret*, capable of transporting 600 tons. Arthur O'Dea of Kinvara also bought barley for Guinness' Breweries in Dublin. Another major buyer of barley was the Galway-based Belfast merchant, Edward McGivern, who purchased through his local agent, Michael Corless, who is wearing a bowler hat recording the tonnage, together with the man inside the tally hut.

A young P.J. Greene (right) sits on a few sacks of barley, wondering, perhaps, if like his father, he too will be agent for Perrse's some day. The Perrses, from whom Lady Augusta Gregory descended, were Cromwellian settlers who made excellent whiskey at their distillery in Nuns' Island, Galway. The whiskey was stored in large yellow casks, or puncheons, which were bigger than porter barrels.

Perrse's distillers purchased barley in Kinvara on Wednesdays and were very particular about the quality of the grain. Barley that appeared in any way damp was refused, and the despondent farmer would have to spread it out again at home to harden it for the next time.

"There is no wine, punch or beer as sweet as the juice of the barley grain" was an old saying in Irish, and most of the older people would have preferred Persse's or Dunville's whiskey. Stout and ale were only making a modest appearance at this time, and right up to the present day, it would still be quite common to see old timers sitting with their half pint of porter and their small one of whiskey.

Photographer unknown
Courtesy of Richard Johnston

THE WINDERMERE SCHOONER c. 1908

The *Windermere,* unloaded and with its sails folded, stretches almost the full length of the pier head. There is not a soul in sight — the waves in the harbour point to a strong north/easterly wind.

John Joe Conneely helped piloting the *Windermere* from Doorus point (or the *Goirmín* anchorage) to the quay, where its cargo of coal was unloaded and barley loaded for the return journey. The ship's last trip to Kinvara is said to have been in the 1930s.

In the 1950s, it was owned by James Tyrell of Arklow. One of the three greatest schooners built in North Wales by A. Ferguson & Son, master boat-builders, it was launched in 1890 at Connah's Quay, Flintshire. A year later this vessel of 179 gross tons (draught: 11 ft.) delivered a cargo of salt to Galway.

At the time it visited Kinvara, the boat would have been owned by the Renay family of Wales. Wooden-built two and three-masted schooners were manned by crews of three to five respectively. In time, merchant schooners would be re-fitted with auxiliary engines, and the *Windermere,* converted to a motor schooner by 1927, was still sailing the channels long after the second world war.

Having collided with the steam trawler, *Father Flynn*, on the Liffey in 1931, the *Windermere* later suffered damage when it went aground at Bristol in 1956. Leaving Cork, it ran into a mud-bank on the river Lee, and finally had to be abandoned when running into difficulties in the Gulf of Lyons, France, in January 1958.

Photographer unknown
Courtesy of Úna Bermingham

Photo: U.S. postcard
Courtesy of Thomas Quinn

TURF DELIVERIES, KINVARA QUAY c. 1905

Turf supplies to Kinvara and Doorus peninsula were as much dependent on weather conditions as were the return trips to Connemara. Boatmen who otherwise were accustomed to rough weather might have had to wait days and sometimes weeks for a gale to abate, especially in the case of a north or north-westerly gale. Hard bargains were driven from time to time, with anxious *bádóirí* (sailors) often having to drop their price in order to catch the tide.

Turf was a labour-intensive source of fuel. From bog to hearth, between footing and loading etc., a sod of turf would be handled about nine times.

The centre hooker, the *Capall* (horse), was built in 1861 by Michael Rainey in Connemara. Skippered by Peter Bailey, the boat is fully laden with turf, yet remains fairly high on the water. His turf came from the Connemara village of Seanaphéistín, noted for its light turf and much in demand at Pat Griffin's forge because of its fast-burning properties.

The shoreline in the background reveals that the quay had yet to be constructed. The children at Céibh a' Céile — possibly the oldest section of the quay — represent the last generation but one of kids who can saunter down to the quay to behold these scenes: to marvel, cajole, pester and, if they are lucky, be chased.

ST ANTHONY'S HOTEL c. 1905

In Kinvara's heyday, the location of St Anthony's Hotel next to the pier made it a popular haunt for boatmen and anyone frequenting the quay.

St Anthony's was a modest guesthouse occupied in the early 1900s by Miss Agnes Flatley, whose father, William, owned most of the adjoining buildings. The property changed hands around 1933, and came into the possession of Nurse Brady.

Behind the hotel was the reputed site of a Huguenot place of worship, founded by William Delamain in the late 1700s. The ruins had been known locally as the 'French Chapel'. In the 1970s, an old church window dated 1782 was uncovered there during development works, and thrown into a hole nearby.

One frequent visitor to St Anthony's was the poet, novelist, and friend of W.B. Yeats, Oliver St John Gogarty, who owned Dunguaire Castle at the time.

By this time, porter was becoming popular. It came in sealed half barrels, the wooden bung being removed and a tap inserted. Having sold their loads of turf, boatmen and customers alike entered St Anthony's for a *béil fhéist* (a treat). Miss Flatley filled a gallon jar (4.5 ltrs) and poured the porter from that. Having bartered and struck a bargain, the customer would buy the boatmen a pint each, as one man recalled: "I drank porter in it. You'd go in for the *béil fhéist*, tenpence a pint. The porter was strong and thick, and your glass would stick to the counter as if it were honey."

35

1995

It is probably a Sunday morning, judging by the closed shutters on Corless's grocery (left) and the small crowd gathered outside Greene's. The poet and author, Francis Fahy, was born here, and by this date will have settled in London, where he is deeply involved in the Gaelic League, and developing his considerable talents. Had fortune decreed differently, he might otherwise have made a significant contribution at home, probably becoming involved in the literary revival movement, which saw its roots to some extent in Kinvara and Doorus around this time.

One day, while en route to visit Baron De Basterot in Parkmore, or her own house, *Mount Vernon* on the Flaggy shore, Lady Augusta Gregory and William Butler Yeats stopped for refreshments in Greene's. They were entertained by 'Missy' Greene, who played for them in the back room on the piano.

All this, however, would be of little relevance to the barefoot child (left) on the untarred road, whose ragged clothing contrasts sharply with the Sunday suits of his peers on the sidecar.

The jarvey holding the reins of the horse is Johnny Lynch. He later lost his right arm in 1914 at the first major offensive of World War 1, and was awarded the Mons Bronze Star Medal. Standing beside the doorway (right) is Mick Traynor, a Connemara man.

"You'd know Connemara men by the way they curled up their hats", one man recalled.

Other identified persons: Child (standing, left): 'Dykie' Burke. Children in sidecar: John, Francis and Patrick Greene. At doorway L-R: Tom Corless (wearing large hat), Thomas Pappy Greene (centre) and Séamus O'Beirne (with cap, right).

GREENE'S HOTEL AND POSTING 1902

Greene's was a posting house as well as an inn. Horses were kept for postriders or for hire by travellers. One could also stable a horse at Greene's or hire a pony and trap. There was a horse called *Terror* that could be in Galway in 40 minutes.

There were four guesthouses, or hotels, in Kinvara: Winkle's, St Anthony's, Corless' and Greene's. Most, if not all of them, could not have survived as hoteliers alone and relied on a supplementary income from the pub, grocery, posting etc.

Photographer unknown
Courtesy of Paddy Greene

FRANCIS FAHY, POET AND PLAYWRIGHT 1854-1935

Francis Arthur Fahy was born on 29 Sept 1854 into a family of 17, eight of whom survived. His father, Thomas, came from the Burren area and his mother was Celia Marlborough, who was born near Gort. A very bright lad at school, he was appointed monitor at Northampton National School in 1866. Three years later he became an assistant teacher in Kinvara Boys School. He was only 15.

That Christmas, 1869, his first play, *The Last of the O'Learys* in which he played the lead role, was performed at Kinvara Courthouse as a fund-raiser for the dependents of Fenian prisoners. The cast included J. St George Joyce, Joseph Fahy and Hyacinth Kilkelly. His poem, *The Exile* was published in the newspaper, *The Nation* on December 24, 1870.

Francis Fahy took a civil service exam and emigrated to England in 1873. In 1878, his father sold the family hotel. Both parents then emigrated to England to live with their son.

While on a return visit in 1889, Francis met his future wife, Agnes Duff from Limerick. His poem, *Maid of Garryowne*, dedicated to her, was published by the *Limerick Leader* that year. They married in the summer of 1891. He was 37 years of age.

They lived in Clapham, London, and Agnes bore four sons, one of whom, Dermot, unveiled the commemorative plaque at Fahy's place of birth in Kinvara (now Griffin's pub) in 1967.

Francis Fahy by all accounts was a very energetic man, fired with enthusiasm and nostalgia for his native country. No sooner had he arrived in England, when, together with others, he founded the Southwark Literary Club, to engender a love of Irish culture amongst the children of Irish emigrants. This became the Irish Literary Society, and later, the Irish Texts Society, being addressed by such luminaries as W.B. Yeats and Bernard Shaw.

In 1886, he became president of the emerging Conradh na Gaeilge (Gaelic League) in London, a position he held until 1908. Described as a small, brisk man, his enthusiasm and energy knew no bounds. He retired from the Civil Service at 65, and died on April 1st, 1935, aged 81.

Francis Fahy's most memorable poems and songs include *The Ould Plaid Shawl, The Queen of Connemara*, the original *Galway Bay*, and *The Tide Full In*. His publications included: *The Child's Irish Song Book* (1881); *The Irish Reciter* (1882); *Irish History in Rhyme* (1882) and *Irish Songs and Poems* (1887).

A VIEW FROM THE SQUARE 1907

Practically all the women in the photo wear the traditional Connemara and Galway shawls, while some of the men are wearing flannel waistcoats. A group stands chatting outside Greene's Hotel, one of the spots where people often congregated. O'Dea's had a grocery and bar next door, where two kilns of porter are visible. A kiln, or half-barrel, had a capacity of 18 gallons (82 litres). The barrel by the wall marks the original iron-gate entrance to the cemetery, which was closed soon after the Famine.

A horse cart of dried *buaileadh isteach* seaweed passes Brigid Bruen's door on its way out of town. In her corner shop, she sold delf, boots and clothes. Greene's (left) and Corless' (opposite) bottled their own porter out of quarter barrels, or firkins, which contained 9 gallons (40.9 litres).

Publicans could also buy bottled beers, wines and sherry etc. from Joe Younge's in Galway, whose porter crates stand outside ready for collection.

Tool handles and scrubheads lean against the entrance to Corless' shop. Beside the (smaller) crates of beer are the empty boxes of dried and salted billy bacon, which was imported from America. Both bacon and box proved very popular, as one man explained: "Them boxes are *American Mate* boxes. The bacon used to come in 9" x 24" slabs (228 x 609 mm); it would be hanging up at the chimney at Christmas, as hard as rock. The boxes could be used when you'd be going to Gort to buy bonnifs (piglets); put on the lid and back you'd come home again. They were very handy."

1995

CORLESS' HOTEL c. 1919

The proprietor of Corless' Hotel, Tom Corless, previously owned a number of hotels in Dublin prior to establishing the hotel business in Kinvara in 1878. Pat Griffin, the blacksmith (left), stands next to young Johnny Shaughnessey, wearing knickerbockers, and another lad holding a whip. This was a popular gable wall for children playing handball. The hotel sign above the trio's heads is a trifle fancier than the one on page 37, and the elaborate rainwater collection system spanning the gable gives a good indication that a mains water supply is not yet available in the village.

A beer crate stands ready for collection on top of two half barrels of porter outside the grocer's shop, which was also an agent for the famous Cunard Line. The Cunard poster board standing against the corner of the building is advertising transatlantic sailings to Canada. Amongst the sailing ships leaving Galway for Quebec a few decades previously in the 1860s were the *Northumberland, Sea Bird, Caractus*, and the *Emma Prescott*.

Tom Corless poses beneath his shop sign, unaware that the arched hotel sign above the adjoining doorway would almost cost him his life. The War of Independence is underway, and the signwriting in Irish, *Teach Ósta Uí Choirléisigh*, did not appeal to the Auxiliaries stationed nearby. Beaten up for refusing to take it down, the soldiers were threatening to shoot him, when the domestic, Mary Donoghue from Spiddal, intervened: "you can shoot me too", she said. The impasse was resolved during the following week when a troubled Mrs Corless had the sign removed.

Children standing in doorway identified as Joe and Mary Corless.

Photographer unknown
Courtesy of Paddy Greene

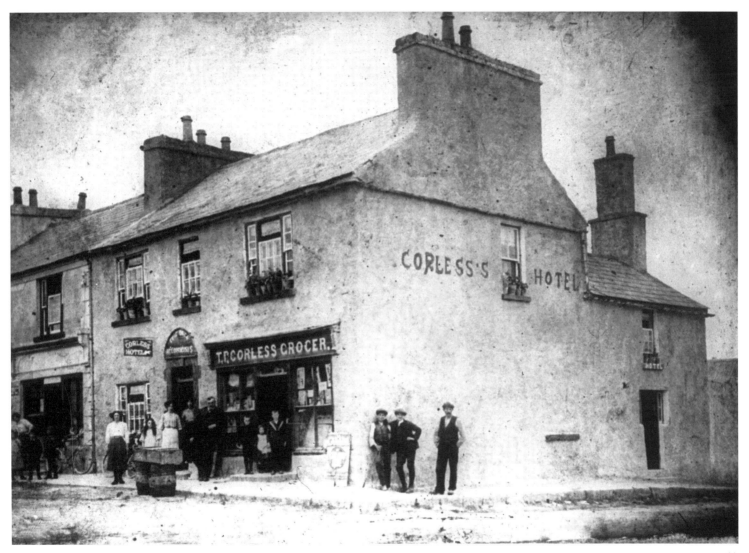

JOHNSTON'S STORE, MAIN STREET c. 1910

At Johnston's store, with its relatively new canopy-holder, a grand selection of household items greets the eye: baths and washtubs, butter churns (on chairs), boots and brooms. Note the sloping, cobbled kerb, and the rack holding the rectangular spades (centre left, resembling a washboard). It was easier, with a horse and cart, to transport both blades and handles separately. Spades needed regular replacement, given the rough limestone terrain in the area.

The prominent display of suitcases shows that emigration was still much the norm. Johnston's were agents for the Cunard, White Star, Dominion and American Lines.

Like most stores, Johnston's was a licensed premises. Whiskey such as Jameson's, Powers and Perrse's were more popular than porter. An eightpenny glass of whiskey would make a half pint of (hot) punch. Women sitting inside might well have covered their heads discreetly with their shawls, had the young lad (left) or anyone else popped their heads in the door.

Johnston's was a general draper, grocer and ironmonger and, it was said, sold anything from a needle to an anchor. When the store closed down in the early 1940s, Fred Johnston travelled the countryside selling off his stock. It was soon refurbished and used as a dance-hall and cinema, with Richie, his son, taking over. In the early 1970s, the hotel became a thriving independent hostel, run by Richard Johnston.

In the 1940s, Johnston's hall was ideal for the *hops,* or dances, as one man recalled: "We used to go to the *fourpenny hops,* they'd let you stay awhile, then clear the hall and you'd have to pay in again. Otherwise you'd stay all day!" Admission to the Sunday night dances was half a crown; set dancing and waltzes were very popular.

Strolling players such as Anew McMaster also staged plays here from time to time up to the 1950s.

In 1949 Gerry Ryan started using Johnston's as a picture house. Paddy Greene remembered that day: "The first film shown there was Keys of the Kingdom with Gregory Peck; Annie O'Donnell cried all the way through — We couldn't hear a thing..."

Fred Johnston in doorway.

Paper shopping bag, ca. 1915.

Photographer unknown
Courtesy of Richard Johnston

The 'Firday Market', 1995.

THE CORN MARKET 1906

The countless carts, 'heeled' up as far as the eye can see on the main street through Kinvara, give a good indication of the sheer magnitude of barley grown in the surrounding countryside at the turn of the century. It is a Wednesday in the month of September, 1906, and the queue of carts stretches all the way down to the quay, where the grain will be checked by Henry Persse's agents and loaded into seven or eight boats. It will be a long day's wait.

Farmers from Turloughmore, Gort, Ardrahan and Craughwell and elsewhere have been arriving since two o'clock in the morning to be amongst the first in line at the quayside. Townspeople trying to get some sleep would be none to pleased, but well-used to the rolling cartwheels, 'clip clop' of horses' hooves and voices of men congregating outside their doorsteps.

Apart from the busy activity on the quay, the village, too, was alive with trade. Taking a walk up the road, one would have passed the business premises of tailors, grocers, bakers, as well as a forge and a hotel. Ballo (Bartholomew) Winkle later had the tolls and customs for the village. On fair days, tollgates or 'gaps' were positioned at vantage points on the Galway, Corrofin, and Ballyvaughan roads, the charge being sixpence for sheep and ninepence for cattle. Tollage ceased in the 1950s.

Just beyond the three men who are standing perfectly in line (left) was James Kilkelly's corner shop. The solitary figure seated outside on a rock was known as 'Ounce' Keane. This corner building had served 20 years previously as the Temperance Hall, established by Father Newell. It was a centre for meetings and band rehearsals, and a starting point for parades led by men on horseback. Alcohol abuse was a big problem in the mid-1800s, when barley was much in demand by the poteen-makers in particular. A barrel (16 stone) of barley would make eight gallons of *poitín*.

Looking up at the photographer is Pat Winkle (foreground, left), wearing the Spanish hat, though 'Big Mac' Maher, the RIC man on his left, seems more interested in the Madden brothers, Joe and Martin, who are rushing by with their box of fish (centre).

"A penny a *wan* (one)" cries Máirín Rourke, with her tray of apples (right).

Also identified: James Kilkelly beside policeman's (with hard hat), and a Nolan from Curranroo to Kilkelly's left. Beside the Madden brothers: their mother Mary (in shawl), and in Flatley's doorway (left) Agnes Flatley.

Photographer: Simmon's Photographers, Galway, or Tomás Ó hEidhin.
Courtesy of Radio Teilfís Éireann

HOME FROM THE WELL c. 1905

It was mostly the older women, reportedly, who carried the buckets on their heads. As in other countries, padding was worn to cushion the weight. The bucket carried on this lady's head would have been hand-made by a travelling tinker.

Wells could run dry in hot summers and with no piped water at home, water was used most sparingly. It may take quite some time in summer before water, trickling into a well, will deliver even a bucketful. Children are told to hasten to the local well very early in the morning to be the first to get the daily supply for the house.

Water being vital, wells were properly cared for, and low walls constructed to keep cattle out; fallen leaves and suchlike were removed. In the case of some (holy) wells, it was not uncommon to find simple offerings like rosaries or medallions nearby. Coins were also thrown into the well by supplicants or hidden nearby. Two wells claimed to be beneficial for eye-ailments were Poll *or* Bullaun Dubhda at Doorus tidal mill and St Colman's Well at Dunguaire, at which rounds of prayers *(pattern)* were conducted annually on 29 Oct.

In her youth, the lady pictured here, Mrs Forde, had been in service at Flatley's, main street. Her people were coopers in Ennistymon. Most of the older persons shown this photograph had seen women carrying buckets in this fashion and remarked also that carrying a stone of flour on your head left both hands free to carry home two shopping bags, one in each hand: "I used to see it in my townland and up above. They used to make a ring of the towel and she'd walk away as grand as anything. Weren't it wonderful when you think of it..."

Mrs Jane Forde, Kinturla townland, Doorus.

Photographer unknown
Courtesy of Thomas Quinn

Saint Ciarán's Bed, 1995.

Saint Ciarán's Bed Trácht, c. 1910

St Ciarán is the patron saint of Doorus peninsula and is said to have arrived at Trácht beach from Inishmore, Aran Islands. Other saints in Doorus include Briocán and Dubhda. Tradition tells of a road opening up in the sea at *Árainn na Naomh* (Aran of the Saints) and closing again upon the arrival of the saint and his followers at Trácht beach. So numerous were they, that the last man was just leaving Inishmore when the message arrived back by word of mouth from Trácht that the saint had left a book behind.

Most of the holy wells around Kinvara were visited on certain dates, and reputedly had curative powers, as did Ciarán's Bed *(Leaba Chiaráin)*, by far the most venerated site in the district. An annual pilgrimage took place to Ciarán's Bed on Garland, or Garlic Sunday (29 July), and hundreds of devotees, both adults and children, would arrive on the previous night.

Pilgrims came from as far away as Portumna, bringing sods of turf to keep themselves warm during the night. Prayers were recited overnight at the saint's bed. The (clockwise) 'patterns' *(patrúin)*, or rounds, continued in the morning, a part of which involved crawling along on one's knees and washing oneself in the sea nearby, as Ciarán is believed to have done. Then, during the afternoon on Garland Sunday, the fun and sport commenced, with boat racing, field races, singing and dancing in a nearby field.

In the picture is Máirtín Conole, of Crushoa, possibly one of the workmen who, having completed "a little altar" at this site in 1910, saw what was described in the *Connaught Tribune* as blood appearing below the altar and on some stones nearby. The large statue of St Ciarán, financed by one Mrs Curtin, was later erected behind this altar.

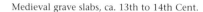
Medieval grave slabs, ca. 13th to 14th Cent.

St Coman's Church c. 1910

Arriving in Kinvara by boat in the Middle Ages, one would have encountered two imposing sites: Dún Guaire Castle on one's left, and a rather striking church on the right. The church known today as St Coman's is said to have been built in the 1540s on the site of a much earlier church, sacked around the year 540 by a marauding band, led by the brothers Ua Carra:

> *We slew the priests that could not flee*
> *We gathered altar, bench, and door,*
> *Mitres and vestments fair to see*
> *We heaped them high, and hurriedly*
> *We burned them on the blood-stained floor*

Years later, the brothers repent of their sins, and are ordered by St Finian of Clonard to make amends and restore all the churches they have ransacked. This they do — except for one — and on reporting back to the saint, he tells them to finish the job:

Photographer: Tomás Ó hEidhin

"...all the churches is built except one,
far distant down in Kinvara shore...
Go hin, *said he, and far away,*
To far Kinvara travel fast
And by St Caimín's church by Galway Bay
Is not the house you'll have to say, you'll leave
around to the last...
That's all I have of it."

This second verse, recited by a local, Crushua man in his 80s, differs somewhat to the original translated version by T.D. Sullivan and gives a good example of how words and versions of local history will change in folk memory, according to the teller and the time. And so it may be with Coleman and Coman. Whether they were kinsmen or one and the same person as suggested by the historian, Monsignor Jerome Fahey, is still a matter for conjecture. Caimín, however, is believed to have been the original saint.

St Coleman, a contemporary if not a relation of Guaire, King of Connacht and patron of the Church, would have had some contact with the earlier church on this site; it certainly provided a convenient place of worship for the residents of Dún Guaire nearby. The major ecclesiastical sites founded by St Coleman in the area were Cill Mac Duach, and Ucht Máma.

After the Reformation, when Church property became Protestant-owned, Catholics were denied access to St Coman's church. Burial of Catholics in the cemetery was also proscribed by the Penal Laws.

The medieval grave slabs (left) date to the 1300s. Uncovered during an inspection in 1987, they represent an important find, establishing the long history of this all-but-forgotten site.

49

St. Coleman's Church, 1995.

Sanctuary, 1988.

SANCTUARY, ST COLEMAN'S CHURCH c. 1920

Kinvara's parish chapel, St Coleman's, was built on land donated by Count De Basterot, and dedicated in 1819. The construction was presided over by Dr. Archdeacon, the Catholic bishop resident in Kinvara at the time, and much of the stone reputedly came from the older church at Mountcross, Moy, about two miles away.

This photograph of the chancel was taken on the occasion of the mission stations, which were held every three years or so.

Much care has gone into preparing the church for the mission. The improvised pulpit (right) and the brass candlesticks and cross (left) together with the timber frame and candle-holders adorning the Virgin Mary, make for a dramatic spectacle for the weeks ahead.

The Redemptorist missions were held during Lent or Autumn, with one week being allocated to men and one week to women. The first Mass of the day would start at 6 a.m., followed by confessions throughout the day, and Mass again in the evening. Each day saw sermons being delivered on specific topics, and the church-bells tolled for the *lost souls* or for those failing or unable to attend. Father Conneely was one of the order of Redemptorists who gave a resounding variety of sermons, and youngsters invariably looked forward to his spiritual discourses on the temptations of the flesh.

Behind the ornamental canopy, or baldachin, hung a large oil painting of the crucifixion by Count James De Basterot himself. The timber galleries along both sides of the chapel were removed around 1951.

The present altar originally came from Galway Pro-Cathedral, and was donated in 1968 by Mary Staunton.

Since its establishment, the parish church, much-revered by its parishioners at home and abroad, has undergone many renovations.

In the 1940s, Monsignor Leech raised money in Stamford, Connecticut, USA, for the restoration of Coleman's church. He compiled a booklet on Kinvara's ecclesiastical sites, and distributed this in his fund-raising drive.

Photographer: Tomás Ó hEidhin

Photographer unknown
Courtesy of Thomas Quinn

BEFORE THE WAR OF INDEPENDENCE c. 1917

A solitary RIC man stands at the corner of Corless's Hotel as packs of wool are conveyed by cart down to Flatley's warehouse.

Across the road, a man wearing a bowler hat buys some fish outside Michael Corless's general provisions store.

The taller building next door was Corless' bakery. There were five bakeries in Kinvara at the time: Michael Corless, Fergus O'Dea, Tyrells, Bartley Bermingham, and Martin O Grady Snr.

The room with the barred window (left) served as a sub-office of the National Bank in the 1940s. It opened for business on Wednesdays mornings, while its major competitor, the Munster & Leinster Bank, opened another sub-office in Greene's across the road. Before that, however, the long narrow room was used by the Garda Síochána. In 1924, following the Civil War, it was used as the temporary day room until such time as the old Protestant school (opposite Community Centre, right) was converted to become the first Garda barracks in Kinvara.

Two details in the picture, though scarcely visible, are noteworthy: in the background, the original Seamount House, obscured by trees, with the large barn, destined for development by the Sisters of Mercy. The other feature is the remains of the entrance to St Coman's church and cemetery, located on the wall adjoining Brigid Bruen's corner shop (gabled, centre left). It may be this very cemetery, closed before the turn of the century, which gave this part of the main street its name: Sráid a' Phúca. Meaning *sprite,* or possibly *phantom* street, the name may be derived from the fact that the lower houses on the left were built, in the early 1800s, over a section of the cemetery.

WATERING THE HORSES AT DUNGUAIRE CASTLE c. 1915

Horses drink their fill near Dunguaire Castle, at a point where the Gort River flows into the sea. The men are working 'in co' (joining forces), sharing horses in the springtime, their own labour at harvest-time.

Their horses are harnessed but the absence of a ploughback seems to indicate that they are not going ploughing. It is a fine, sunny evening; possibly they have finished for the day.

An observant farmer, pointing to the horses' ribs, remarked that this photo would have been taken around March, a hungry time of the year for animals, as growth had not yet begun.

To the right of the horsemen is the clemeen pier, where harvested seaweed was brought ashore.

The roofless castle stands empty and desolate. Sows are kept in the courtyard beyond the castle gate.

This scene reminded more than one person of the Wild West: "We used to play cowboys and indians there in the '30s...talk about the Rio Grande..."

In the early 1960s, the eccentric Lady Ampthill purchased the ruin of Dunguaire Castle from the author and playwright, Oliver St John Gogarty. A descendant of a decaying aristocracy, Lady Ampthill was often seen riding side-saddle through the village, and her two hounds always sat in her car wherever she went. She brought local children on field trips, was accustomed to giving brusque orders to domestic staff and expected immediate compliance, but was kindly nevertheless, and generally liked by the locals. When she died in the 1970s, she was cremated and according to her wishes, her ashes were scattered over the castle. The castle was later purchased by the Shannon Development Company and is open to the public.

Pat Winkle (left) and unidentified companion.

Photographer: Christy Greene

Photographer unknown
Courtesy of Tom Leech

LEECH'S BUTCHER STALL c. 1925

Kinvara had four butchers' shops, known as 'stalls'. Meat was delivered by suppliers from the Gort area, though most butchers slaughtered their own stock.

Leech's victuallers were established in 1903. Thomas Leech (right, in doorway) was a lime, timber and iron merchant as well. He worked also as a part-time contractor, doing repair works on the causeway at Aughinish, Doorus, and on other projects around the town of Kinvara.

Carcasses such as these two sides of mutton hanging outside Leech's shop were kept open with sticks for presentation purposes. The mutton was occasionally basted with blood (as opposed to colouring today) to make it more attractive for the customer. Butchers regularly displayed beef, pork and poultry outside their shops in this fashion, a practice which ceased in the early 1970s.

Some children could not resist the temptation of passing butchers' stalls without leaving their mark. Using the tongue of an old leather boot, they'd give the bluebottles buzzing on the carcass a good whack, leaving them embedded in the meat.

Other identified persons: Mrs Ann Leech, next to her husband, Thomas. Their children, Annie, holding dog; Michael (left), Mikey Joe Leech (doorway) and Katie Leech.

Photographer unknown
Courtesy of Paddy Connolly

CONNOLLY'S FORGE c. 1920

It is said that there were about eight blacksmiths in Kinvara at the turn of the century. This is not surprising, given the scale of business in the town at the time. The busy activity at the quay was augmented by the various markets and the great number of horse, cattle, sheep and pig fairs held annually, all of which provided spin-off employment for craftsmen like masons, blacksmiths and carpenters.

For the farmer, horse and donkey carts were indispensable, as were other farm accessories, such as the timber or iron plough, harrows, gates, wheelbarrows, and other hand-held implements for digging drills, forking hay etc.

Paddy Connolly (left) had a forge and a carpenter's workshop side by side. Amongst his employees were a number of young men who had received their initial training in an industrial school.

Busy as he was, the blacksmith was not a rich man. Farmers often had no money to pay him and sometimes would be obliged to bring the next job to another smith in town, as the blacksmith was damned if he was going to do a second job on tick as well.

Neither was the forge a very healthy working environment. Blacksmiths occasionally suffered from chest complaints, chiefly from coal dust, as one man explained: "Jackeen went to England once — you know when you throw out a spit and it comes out white — well in the forges those days it would be black. Well I'll tell you how bad it was, now. Jackeen went to England and when he came back a month later his spit was still black. That's how bad it was..."

Still, the forge was a great meeting point for men and boys, as the pump or well would have been for women. The blacksmith was a highly respected craftsman too. He had all the elements at his command — earth, fire and water, and often acted as the arbiter in the settling of local disputes. The forge water itself was said to have a cure.

Left to right: Paddy Connolly, Richie Burke, Mattie Regan, Unidentified person, John McCormack, Brigid Staunton, John MacMahon.

Photographer unknown
Courtesy of Finola Murphy

REPAIRING SAILS; KINVARA QUAY
c. 1919

The picture captures a quieter moment in the lives of men whose existence revolves around the sea, where maintenance work invariably attracted company, leading to banter and gossip.

A sail is spread out on the footpath for repair, as Tom Moran, the bay pilot (bearded) looks on. In front of him, working on the sail, is his successor, John Joe Conneely, together with Thomas Conneely. The Conneely clan were claimed in folklore to have descended from the seals, and therefore to have a strong bond with the sea.

The wooden stairs on the gabled building in the distance, led upstairs to where the William O'Brien Fife and Drum Band practised. The band had about 20 members, and must have made a fine impression at sports' events and festivals, with their fifes, side drums, and kettle drums,

Other bay pilots were Pádraig (Rory) Greene and Séamus Ward, who ferried sailors ashore in his rowing boat, *The Galley*. Preceding them all was Martin Corless in 1867.

On one occasion, the bay pilots were sick, and one lad, a part time pilot, was asked if he could guide the schooner, the *Gaelic,* into harbour. Not one to miss an opportunity, he boasted:. "I know every rock in the bay." On their way into Kinvara, they struck a rock near the pier. The shocked Scottish sea captain asked:

"I thought you knew every rock?"

"I do, Sir, that was one of them!"

Also in photo: Pádraig Mac Donncha, on Tom Moran's left, wearing hat.

STEAMSHIP AT KINVARA QUAY 1918

The Limerick Steamship Company, with a base in Galway docks, delivers a cargo to Kinvara, still a moderately busy port at this time. The big ship extends far beyond the pier head and will need to unload its cargo quickly before the tide turns, or remain grounded for 12 hours.

Large vessels such as this steamship delivering coal and possibly iron were guided into Kinvara port by a pilot. As return freight, some carried pine staves destined for the Welsh mines.

Coal was transported as far away as Loughrea by horse and cart, for which the delivery man was paid half a crown per ton loaded. Shovelling black coal all day, an arduous, dusty job, earned one man working on the boat the nickname 'Coal-box'.

Aside of the Flatleys who imported coal, the phosphate-rich fertiliser, guano, was also imported in two-hundredweight bags by local merchants like the Murphy's and O'Deas.

A famous steamship coming to Kinvara in the early 1900s was the *Dun Aonghus*, which also served the Aran Islands prior to the *Naomh Éanna*. The *Dun Aonghus* sailed on summer excursions from Galway to Ballyvaughan, arriving in Kinvara perhaps three times during the summer. It would stay about 2 hours, and sail on the tide. The loud steam-siren announcing her departure terrified local children. For a time it also came once weekly to Kinvara with provisions, mainly Palmer's Flour, but this was discontinued when it proved uneconomical.

Photographer:
Tomás Ó hEidhin

THE HYNES AND THE HANBERRYS OF DUNGUAIRE c. 1906

Times of peace: The photographer from Killina townland, Tomás Ó hEidhin, would have been about 24 years old when he took this photograph. The marriage of his (bearded) brother, Patsy Hynes, to Sally Dunne (standing) brought the family name back to their ancestral home, near Dunguaire Castle.

Sally's sister, Mainie, who is seated in front of her, married her next door neighbour, Tim Hanberry. She is flanked by her daughters, Brigid and Katie.

Brigid married Tom Connolly of Gortaboy townland. Katie emigrated to Connecticut, America, in the early 1920s, along with her cousin next door, Willy Hynes. Mary and another brother, Mikey, were the last of the Hynes to live in the house. They never married.

VOLUNTEERS POSING BESIDE RUINS OF HYNES' HOUSE Nov 1920

All but one of these men were to see their family homes destroyed by the Auxiliaries.

In November 1920, the Hynes' home near Dunguaire Castle was burnt to the ground by the Auxiliaries. Nothing survived but a clock. Mikey and Willy Hynes were active IRA volunteers, and were on the run at the time.

The Hynes family moved into their barn, and it was here, one week later, that the charred and multi-bayoneted remains of the Loughnane brothers from Shanaglish — Pat and Harry — would be waked.

Missing for 10 days, any knowledge of these "escaped prisoners" had been denied by the Auxiliary Division, stationed at Drumharsna Castle. However, several persons, including a remorseful constable, who reputedly told where the bodies could be found, had witnessed what must have been one of the worst unpunished atrocities in the entire war. The grim task of laying out the broken bodies fell to local members of *Cumann na mBan*, the IRA's sister organisation — Mary Hynes, her cousin Katie Hanberry (see photo left) and Onnie Duane, sister of Joe Kilkelly.

Soon after, the Auxiliaries, on discovering the Loughnanes were waked in the Hynes' barn, burnt that also. Patsy moved into the shed, Sally and Mary to the Hanberrys next door. The new house was completed in 1924.

Right (L-R): Joe Kilkelly, Crushoa, (later went to USA) Pádraig Fahy, local IRA commander, Mikey Hynes (aged 21) and Séamus Davenport.

Photographer:
Tomás Ó hEidhin

TRICOLOUR FLIES OVER DEMOLISHED RIC BARRACKS
July 1920

This photograph shows the abandoned RIC barracks after it was torn down on the night of 20 July 1920 by the Kinvara Company of the IRA, led by Captain John Burke. Fire would have spread to adjoining buildings, so ropes and sledgehammers were used to pull it down. Such attacks were intended to prevent re-occupation by the Crown Forces.

The period January 1919 to March 1920 saw over 20,000 raids by the Crown Forces in Ireland. IRA attacks — sporadic or consistent, depending on local conditions — were seriously undermining British rule. By May 1920 the number of evacuated barracks destroyed or partially damaged totalled 456. In country areas, the constabulary abandoned village stations for the relative safety of larger towns, as did the 11 RIC men, or 'peelers', stationed in Kinvara.

In March 1920 the dreaded Black and Tans arrived in Ireland, followed a month later by the Auxiliary division. The 'Tans' and the 'Auxies' were, respectively, veteran soldiers and ex-officers of the 1914-18 war. Their job was to crush the slightest resistance.

The War of Independence (Jan 1919-July 1921) saw terrible atrocities committed by all sides. In September 1920, an IRA ambush just outside Kinvara was foiled when the Constabulary failed to show. Suspected informers were shot and "traitors beware" pinned to their chests. In August, a constable Duffy was shot dead near Tubber; other policemen were killed and wounded in an ambush at Castledaly in October. The RIC rarely knew when or where the IRA would strike next. Officially-sanctioned reprisals by the Crown forces were commonplace: houses and crops were set alight; looting and summary executions were condoned.

Photographer: Tomás Ó hEidhin

SEAMOUNT COLLEGE: HUMBLE BEGINNINGS 1922

Pictured are the original junior and senior pupils enroled in Seamount College. Seamount House and lands had been bequeathed by Mrs Elisabeth Nally-Hynes to the Sisters of Mercy. The Order was anxious to put the building, which had been vacant for some time, to immediate use. Tyrone House, near Kilcolgan, had been burnt some years previously during the War of Independence.

With the Civil War raging at this time, the nuns were fearful for the safety of Seamount House. Plans were put in train and what was later to become a prestigious college and boarding school opened its doors for the first time on the feast of Our Lady of Mercy, 24 September 1922.

The younger children seen here were accommodated according to age in St Joseph's National School and St Joseph's Convent in Kinvara village. Those children wearing sashes were consecrated Children of Mary, a special devotion to the Blessed Virgin very popular at that time. Tilly Hayes (back row, 2nd left) and most of the other girls in the picture became nuns in later life.

The Sisters of Mercy continued to make improvements to the college and by 1926 they were able to cater for all secondary school grades as well as provide accommodation for boarders. The college had been given full recognition by the educational authorities and by 1931 the numbers attending had risen to 45. That year also saw the introduction of their own electric power plant, installed on the Feast of Our Lady of Lourdes. A chapel was constructed and opened in 1932, the year of the Eucharistic Congress in Dublin. Hand-painted stations were purchased in Paris and financed by the widow of a wealthy expatriate, Willy Brennan. Further extensions were built according to necessity, with the present three-storey building being completed in September, 1938. The college continued to expand both in attendance and reputation. For many years, it was the only secondary school for girls in the general district. Boys were at a disadvantage and would have required scholarships to attend St Mary's College in Galway, a fee-paying institution. Either that or cycle in all weathers the 15 km to Gort to attend the two-year course in the VEC technical school, which opened in 1940.

Rita (Missy) Greene, far back, on right.

THE SISTERS OF MERCY, KINVARA

The sisters shown here were installed in Tuam and often visited their parents, the Lynchs, in Kinvara. The seated couple were the grandparents of the late Joe Lynch, Main St, Kinvara. As members of the Sisters of Mercy order, their daughters would also have visited the Convent Church of St Joseph, established some 40 years earlier.

Founded in 1878, this huge undertaking was made possible by donations from the wealthy Galway merchants, William Murray of Northampton House, and Captain Blake Foster of Castle Foster (Doorus Demesne), both of whom had endowed money and granted land respectively.

On a fine, sunny day in April, 1878, a paddle steamer, the *Cittie of the Tribes*, chartered by way of donation by a Mr Guilfoyle, landed at the quay in Kinvara. The steamer with its 300 passengers had arrived from Galway for the celebratory inauguration which was also to be addressed by the famous preacher, Father Tom Burke O.P. Others had come by road for the occasion.

On board the steamer on this festive Sunday morning were the St Patrick's Temperance Society Brass Band and a string band comprising members of the temperance society. They played during the voyage, each band at either end of the steamer, and on the quay upon arrival. Both bands then paraded up the town followed by a large crowd, where they were met by the Gort Total Abstinence Society Band.

After Mass, the celebrated Dominican Father preached his resounding sermon to a crowd estimated at 4,000, and the *Cittie of the Tribes* made its return trip at about 3 p.m. Coinciding with this grand event was the opening of Corless' Hotel, which provided the catering for the occasion.

St Joseph's National School, the primary school attached to St Joseph's Convent, was then established in 1904. It could cater for 400 pupils, and the entire undertaking was recognised as both significant in terms of the Church's influence in the area and as a resource for the education of future generations of children in the parish. The convent eventually transferred to Seamount and the school to an adjacent building. The building then served as St Joseph's church, with a presbytery alongside.

Photographer: Christy Greene

MARY FAHY

Living in the corner building opposite Leech's victuallers, (see page 54), was Mary Fahy, who sold apples and plums, gooseberries and nuts when they were in season. She was also called *Máire bodhar*, owing to her partial deafness.

Only half the building, described as a ruin, or a 'cowl' *(cabhail)* was occupied by her. The other half was roofless. Her corner was known as 'Fahy's Corner', and her gabled building was one of the favourite spots in the village for children playing handball. Children sometimes would trick her by throwing pebbles at the shop. While she chased them, others ran in and grabbed some fruit for themselves.

Her father sold kid goats in his time, as popular a meal for the Easter dinner as goose was for Christmas.

Mary Fahy was described as being of a very sallow complexion. She died tragically in old age after falling into the fireplace.

KINVARA POST OFFICE c. 1924

The post office in Kinvara was opened in 1833 as a sub-office of Ardrahan. Postage costs were prohibitive for many at first but by 1840, it became possible to send a letter for one penny.

In August 1894, the first delivery service in Kinvara took place in the town itself and Martin Traynor became the Village Deliverer.

A rural delivery to Doorus House, near Trácht, commenced in 1898. The service then expanded gradually to the countryside, spreading to Northampton in 1901 and to Aughinish in 1907.

Prior to the arrival of the Safety Bicycle, postmen had to do their rounds on foot, walking some 20 km a day. In 1905, Michael Staunton was provided with the first official bicycle in Kinvara. He was paid 7/6 (37½ new pence) per week, plus one shilling for cleaning his bike.

Mail originally had been collected by Post Boys or by the Ennis Mail Car, and later, on contract by horse and sidecar. With the birth of the Free State in 1922 came the establishment of the Department of Posts and Telegraphs, and later, its own motor mail van from Galway, with a postman as the driver.

The telephone exchange in Kinvara was opened in 1925, with calls going through the local post office. An automatic exchange was provided in 1981, after which local numbers changed. In 1979, the number for a local guesthouse, for example, was Kinvara 34.

Mary Phelan, pictured here, was the longest serving postmistress in Kinvara. She started in May 1922, two months after the death of her husband, John Phelan, who had been postmaster for two years. Following her retirement in 1961, she was replaced by Miss Frances Ryan. Francie Ryan's post office was next door to Leech's craft shop. Mary Phelan's post office was situated at the fork on the Gort road, close to today's post office, managed by another generation of the Ryans.

Photographer: Christy Greene

THE KINVARA HORSE RACES

The Gortshanvogh races held in the 1920s on Johnston's land (near St Coleman's parish church) were renowned throughout Ireland, and advertised as far away as Delgany in Co Wicklow. Races were held from July to September, when hay had been cut in the meadows, and the time for sports days and festivities had begun.

Kinvara Race Committee officials and stewards comprised both traders and others living near the town. A local doctor usually presided as judge at the races. Subscriptions were collected by the race committee to finance the cash prizes, and the various trophies sponsored included The Traders' Plate, the Stewards' Plate, and the Volunteer Plate.

A poster advertising the 1890 event specifies that the previous year's winner of the coveted Kinvara Plate, if taking part, would have to carry 14 lbs (6.3 kg) extra weight. The 1888 winner had to carry double that amount. It was not known whether races were held before 1888.

The Kinvara Plate later became the prestigious Galway Plate, awarded nowadays at the famous Galway Races, a landmark signalling the holiday season for rural communities in the West.

The *Tuam News* of 2/8/1889 reported that the races that year at Gortshanvogh (Gort Sean Bhó — field of the old cow) attracted 5,000 people. Those in attendance were entertained by a group of violinists and a highland piper, the paper noted. Also, the poet Francis Fahy, alias *An Dreoilín* (the wren), sang a few songs to the delight of the audience. It continued: "The fair sex, decked in their gayest attire, mustered in great strength, much to the joy of young men graduating in the school of cupid."

Amongst the names telegraphed by the Irish Racing Association in Dublin as entries for what may have been the last Kinvara race in 1923, were *Silver Ring, Cow Boy, Lisdoonvarna Lass, Hot Stuff, Black Chicken,* and *Pretty Polly*.

Some people were reluctant to attend the Kinvara races, owing to their tattered clothing. They chose instead to watch from a hill across the road which became known as *Cnoc na nGiobóg* (Hill of the Ragged).

On posters of the period, a notice proscribes the game of 'Aunt Sally'. Described as a side event, this dangerous game was possibly the precursor of the shooting gallery at fairgrounds. Inside a 45 gallon barrel with a spyhole near the top, was a lad, whose job it was to pop his head up and down. Your job, of course, was to hit him with one of the four sticks (batons) you paid for. The young lad had to watch out in particular for the devious left-handed punter whose luring right-handed throw was followed instantly with a cracking aim from his left.

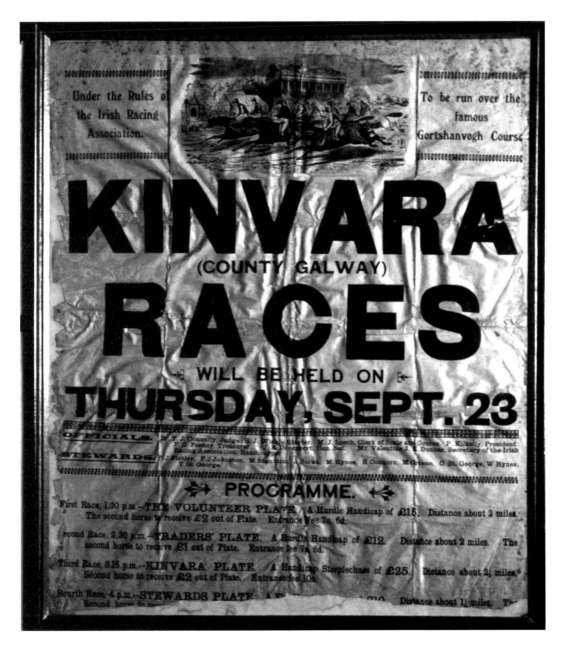

BECALMED QUAY c. 1927

The absence on the quay of the general hustle and bustle depicted in other photographs has more to do with changing fortunes than with a low tide. Aside of the *Zulu* and *gleoiteóg* — possibly in Kinvara on a simple errand such as a visit to the forge — there is little evidence of what one might expect from a busy seaport town. Turf fragments on the quay (left), and the remnants of a bank of turf on the pier indicate however that turf, at least, is still coming ashore.

The civil unrest in the wake of the 1922 Treaty, which led to the formation of the Free State, left its mark on the economy of Kinvara, as it did elsewhere. Railway lines had been blown up during the Civil War, disrupting the economic infrastructure on which market towns and ports like Kinvara depended. Terminal decline was to follow.

A man passes opposite Davenport's, whose house was burned by the Auxiliaries in 1919. The last house on the right was used as a picture house and for travelling shows. It was partly demolished in the 1970s to widen the corner. Next door is St Anthony's Hotel, with a gabled extension called 'Bradley's wing'. The adjoining lane, where the Flatleys reputedly kept a horse and sidecar in the past, was said to be haunted; some accounts told of a *taibhse* (phantom) who would walk down this lane.

At night, Pat, and later, John Holland lit the paraffin lamps, of which one is visible (right). This continued to be done until about 1965. Delamaine Lodge (extreme right), thatched at this time, was slated in the late 1930s by John Ryan.

During the 1700s, a small community of Huguenots of French extraction lived along the shoreline known as the Claddagh. Delamaine Lodge was built by them around 1760, possibly on the site of a collapsed castle. The lucrative, illegal, export of wool is believed to have taken place from here, and traded in France for wines, brandy, tea, and bales of tobacco. A secret tunnel — explored as a child in the early 1900s by a man who remembered hearing cows grazing overhead — is said to have led from the house to the shore for smuggling purposes. Captain William Delamain's links with the south-west of France may have led to his son's marriage to a cognac merchant's daughter in Jarnac. James Delamain sold the Lodge in 1793 and its contents were auctioned.

Photographer unknown
Courtesy of Tommy Corless

THE EMIGRANT SHIP 1929

A German-registered ship, the *Karlsruhe,* prepares to set sail for the land of hope and glory, America, otherwise known as *an t-Oileán Úr* (the New Land).

A sense of expectancy is in the air; passengers link arms in a spirit of solidarity and camaraderie, pushing aside the tears and last goodbyes of the 'American Wake' the night before.

For many of them, the passage money arrived from relatives in the States, and they, in turn, would send the dollars for the next in line.

It may be nearly 20 years before any of these enthusiastic young emigrants can actually afford a return visit to Ireland. By that time many of these Galway-born 'Yanks' would have fared reasonably well in the USA. Their Irish temperament and their rural upbringing had endowed them with a variety of skills and an ability to adapt and survive in a totally new and alien environment.

Difficult times are ahead, however, for they would arrive at the beginning of the Great Depression, a time of mass unemployment and much hardship in the 'States. But they would be met by relatives and friends in cities like Stamford, Boston, New York, Philadelphia and Toronto, who had taken the boat many years before.

Soon to be integrated into the new vibrant community of Irish emigrants, they would become an important influential force in the fabric of American society.

On board this vessel which sailed from Galway in 1929 was a young Michael John Ryan (3rd row extreme left, wearing large hat).

Other identified persons: Paddy Quinn, Moy (3rd row, left, next to Michael J Ryan); Brigid Greene (3rd row, 5th left wearing beret).

Photographer unknown
Courtesy of Gerry Ryan, Kinvara and
Ms Greene, Stamford, Connecticut

MURPHY'S WAREHOUSE c. 1930

Sacks of barley are delivered by farmers to Murphy's warehouse on the quay, to be shipped out in due course. The depot also stored the smaller but equally heavy bags of guano fertiliser, a phosphate-rich manure from Chile in South America. The hitherto substantial market for seaweed as a fertiliser would soon undergo a gradual decline, with other types of manure capturing the market.

The biggest boat ever arriving in Kinvara is believed to have been the *S.S. Mungret*, which could carry 600 tons of barley. Other large vessels docking at the quay included the three-masted schooners, the *Gaelic* and the *Windermere* and the big sailing ship, the *Emerald Isle*.

The *Gaelic* was a three-masted, engine-powered schooner which delivered coal and manure to Kinvara, returning with barley. Upon arrival at Doorus Point, she would drop anchor and await high tide before being piloted into Kinvara quay. Two or three carts were then hired by the consignee to unload the cargo, a logistically cumbersome task which usually took a full week.

If leaving without a cargo, it was necessary for schooners to be loaded with a large amount of stones as ballast.

This three-storey warehouse was built before 1850 and previously owned by the Perrses, who purchased enormous quantities of corn for their distillery in Galway.

Murphy's storage depot was re-roofed in 1940. It also had a kiln drier for barley. A high tide on the quay once flooded the depot, destroying the fertiliser stored there. In 1945, the floors were taken out and the bottom floor raised one metre, to prevent a reoccurrence. Flooding was to occur again, however, in 1961; this time barley was destroyed, and the culprit, Hurricane Debbie.

The sheer weight of these two hundredweight bags (16 stone/100 kilos) is mind-boggling. Yet, men, who had a special way of lifting the large, heavy sacks, were able to carry them on their backs up the ramp into Murphy's.

But did it do their backs any damage? Some people were described as being "bent over in the finish" whereas others, such as Tommy Killeen, lived to be old men. Bartley Mogan's father could carry a bag under each arm, it was said, and Mrs Tyrell, a small woman who had a drapery and grocery store nearby, was often seen carrying an 8 stone bag of flour on her back.

Photographer unknown
Courtesy of Tommy Corless

Photographer unknown
Courtesy of Paddy Greene

MYSTERY OF BOATS ON PIER HEAD 1930s

Questions as to why these boats were up on the pier drew a blank. How they got up there in the first place was a mystery, as it would have been difficult to hoist a solid timber boat onto the pier without a crane. Likewise, the two masts, one of which appears to be rigged, would usually be down when not in use.

It was suggested that the boats were impounded by the Sheriff, but had that been the case, they probably would have been brought to the Claddagh Basin in Galway.

A more plausible theory is that they were on dry dock for maintenance or repair. Special skills were necessary to get the two boats safely out of the water. Choosing one of the very high spring tides in the year, the boats could be slowly manoeuvred onto the pier, using seaweed as a base. By pulling down on the mast, and tilting the boats to 45 degrees or more, they could then be slid over the seaweed onto the pier. The same pulling and sliding techniques could be used at the next high tide to manoeuvre the boats back into the sea, hence the reason for leaving the masts in place.

The *gleoiteóg* or *leath-bhád* against the wall on the right may be a Rainey-built boat. The other boat, closer to the pier-edge might be Keane's boat, built by the other master boat-builder, Patsey Brannely. Seáinín Keane lived nearby in the townland of Cartron and made his living drawing seaweed and fishing herring, which was available in abundance in Galway bay at the time.

SHEEP WASHING NEAR DUNGUAIRE c. 1932

Sheep had to be washed to remove the grease, prior to shearing a day or two later. At the slip and all along the quay and the claddagh — wherever one could find a place to get down — hundreds of sheep were washed in late May and shorn a few days later.

A good man might shear 30 sheep a day. It was hot, thirsty, work and now and again shearers were handed a pint of porter.

Most farmers in the Kinvara area were involved in mixed farming at the time: sheep, cattle and tillage.

Many breeds of sheep were raised in the Kinvara countryside. The Galway ewe and Connemara cheviot were much favoured for their excellent fleeces of wool, as was the mutton of the Cheviot wether.

Attending the numerous annual fairs throughout the county gave sheep farmers the opportunity to expand their horizons and hear the latest news. Having attended fairs since their childhood, they were well-versed in the conventions of deal-making, and wary of the *ceannaí cluaise*, the shifty eavesdropper trying for a quick bargain.

Luck-pennies changed hands, and superstitions, or *pishrogues (pisreogaí)*, though not always believed, were rarely ignored. Good dogs were indispensable to the shepherd, with a sheepdog being prized for attributes such as being a good *creeper,* not being too *hostile* on stock, and a mild dog who is *obedient to the call*.

Shepherds, who could diagnose every bleat, knew much about traditional cures, as did the forerunners of the veterinary profession: the *quacks,* who plied their own, often complex, cures with frequent success.

Photographer unknown
Courtesy of Tommy Corless

ROAD-SURFACING 1929

The dusty smell of broken, crushed rocks mingles with pungent tar and rising steam, as the road-laying process reaches the bottom of the town.

A man tends to Mikey Hynes's horse cart, while Mikey himself spreads rubble with a shovel (foreground). Stones for this major public works scheme had been drawn in this horse cart to the village square, and piled high in the yard behind Corless' pub. The heap of rocks measured some 20 metres long, and 3 metres high. A machine then arrived to crush the rocks used in the road-making operation. Stones were also broken by hand, with men being paid by the ton.

Some of the houses on the right were built in the early 1800s over a cemetery. When shown this photo, a local woman recounted how her ancestors had been troubled by this new development: "My father told me that his father told him, before those houses came into vogue, that skeletons were dug up in the cemetery there. They were piled up in a heap in the corner (left) and they were taken away in a common cart."

Mutton hangs outside Leech's victuallers. The derelict building on the right was used by the butcher for slaughtering kid-goats. Next door is Halloran's drapery, where the customary outdoor display has been removed. The shop opposite, which sold stationary, papers, tobacco, flour and meal, belonged to James Kilkelly, who used to write a column for the *Connaught Tribune*.

Photographer: Christy Greeene

STONE CRUSHER 1930s

Working for half a crown a day, the road-worker's job demanded endurance and toil. The 10 man road gang employed by the County Council had no mechanical conveniences like diggers or lorries at their disposal — just a sturdy, timber-built wheel barrow and a horse cart. Their daily work involved loading rocks, spreading gravel, filling carts and emptying them again, while wearing out their shovels in the process.

All work, therefore, was manual, except for the steam-operated stone-crusher. Stones were hoisted on a strapped conveyor belt (left) to the crusher above, where the graded screen separated and crushed the stone, delivering the gravel in a chute to the workmen below. The steam engine at the rear operated the driving belt connected to the pulleys on the crusher.

The operator, known as the flag-man, or fire-man, was the first to arrive before 8.30 in the morning, to fill the furnace with whatever was available: turf, timber, or especially coal, which was the preferred fuel.

The workmen's hut at the very back afforded shelter in rough weather as well as overnight accommodation for those who did not live in the vicinity, such as the operator himself, who came from the midlands.

The workmen are, from left to right: Christy Ward, Peter McCormack, Mikey Hynes, Paddy Joe Keane, crusher (unidentified), Séamaisín Ward, unidentified person, Paddy McCormack, Tommy Gill, and John Burke (the ganger). Rear: Williameen Ward.

Photographer unknown
Courtesy of Paddy Greeene

1995

STREETSCENE, EUCHARISTIC CONGRESS June 1932

A woman in O'Dea's doorway (left), keeps a watchful eye on the barefoot child crossing the road in the wake of 'the sweetman', Geary's from Limerick, which delivered sweets, *currant tops* and *penny biscuits* to the village shops.

The street is bedecked with papal flags and bunting in honour of the Papal Nuncio's visit to Ireland, a momentous event in Ireland that year. A banner, partially legible in Irish, stretches across the street, and praises the glory of God.

Wool and various garments hang on display outside O'Halloran's drapery shop, with rolls of oil cloth and other fabrics stacked on crates and barrels along the quiet, main road.

The man standing at the doorway of Lynch's grocery store looks on, bemused as determined youth passes him by. Lynch's was also a popular public house and later became a local branch of the Galway County libraries in the 1960s.

Annie Leech, noted for her fine singing voice in the church choir and her lucky escape during the great San Francisco earthquake in 1906, sold sweets and cigarettes next door. Brigid Bruen's corner shop sold tanned leather, boots and clothes. Up the road, a man is casually driving two cows up the town, where most of the older buildings are thatched. The shawled woman outside Corless's pub (left) most likely is selling fish.

1995

LEAVING TOWN 1932

Bunting and flags in honour of the Eucharistic Congress tell the date of this photograph. The ruins of the RIC barracks serve as a reminder of the Troubles 13 years earlier.

Across the street stands a building belonging to Peter Feeney, a family grocer and part-time undertaker whose son, Vincent, later became Mayor of Limerick. Feeney's had been a general smithworks, funeral and posting establishment, and advertised itself also as an agent for Thompson's celebrated corsets. When a fire had broken out here some years before, people formed a human chain as far as the quay, filling buckets. There was a full tide at the time, but it did not save the building.

Eddie Tyrell's car is parked outside his mother's drapery store (now Brogan's shop). He ran a taxi service, often ferrying the Sisters from the convent at Seamount (behind trees) to and from the convent in Gort. The original entrance to the convent was situated at the corner wall, just beyond Tyrell's.

Passing the new entrance to Seamount is a horse cart probably heading for Kilcolgan or Ardrahan with its load of dry seaweed.

Crates of Guinness stacked outside Connolly's pub are left there for the delivery man, who comes with a horse and cart. Each crate contained six dozen bottles of porter.

This part of town did good business during fair days and one or two pubs were licensed to open at 6 a.m. on such occasions. Two brothers in particular who frequented the pub were remembered to have a 'terrible' thirst: they would be drinking all day and were known to drink a case of Guinness, 72 bottles, each.

1995

THE KILMACDUAGH ROAD 1932

Also photographed during the Eucharistic Congress celebrations is the southern approach to the village of Kinvara. An important access point for the farmer coming to fairs, or the merchant having business on the quay, the road veered off here at the fork to inland agricultural towns like Gort and Loughrea, Ennis and Corrofin.

The latter approach, the Corrofin road, was also known as the Kilmacduagh road. In medieval times this would have provided a significant link between the major ecclesiastical site at Kilmacduagh, 10 miles away, and St Coman's church, the ruined gable of which still towers above the rooftops, behind Leech's shop (centre). Part of an old cemetery lies beneath a section of the road and some of the adjoining houses blocking this particular view of the early church (see reconstruction, page 13).

The Irish flag hangs above Bridie Leonard's shop (left), while two dogs cavort outside her rather quaint doorway. Birdcages were popular at the time, and the two cages seen here would have housed either goldfinches, larks or thrushes. Two renowned bird catchers in the area were Patrick MacMahon and Johnny Lynch.

Tommy Shaughnessey and his daughter are seated outside their house (right) which until about 1915 had been the village dispensary, and today serves as the post office. Beside the family pub at 'Kathleen Quinn's Corner' (now 'Sexton's Corner'), stands Kathleen Quinn.

Other identified persons: William Ward at corner (right). Left of Ms Quinn is Michael Leech, and the barefoot boy in front of his doorway (foreground, right) is Oliver Ryan, with his baby sister, Chrissie.

THE EGG STORE
HELEBERT'S ON THE QUAY 1930s

Poultry farming contributed significantly to the domestic economy, with turkeys, geese, ducks and hens being raised mostly by the women in the parish.

The sale of eggs to Heleberts and other merchants such as J.Peter O'Grady or Piggotts of Gort gave the housewife the money she needed to pay for tea, sugar, flour and bacon, not to mention a sense of pride in having contributed to the household income.

With help from her children, she might tend to a hundred hens or more. Fowl were fed on wheat and barley or boiled Indian meal mixed with potatoes.

Pat Helebert had a grocery shop beside Regan's on the quay and his egg-grading store was located nearby. He went around the countryside every week with a horse and cart, buying eggs. Eggs were stacked in layers of straw and supplied by the score (20s) to the dealer when he called to the house.

The Department of Agriculture poster on the wall is an indicator of the stringent controls exerted by the authorities at the time.

The intrepid young man with the fag in his mouth was known as Patch Mac. A great men for trapping birds, and selling them, or tinkering with clocks. He later worked as a barber in a little shed outside his home, and was fondly remembered: "He'd stand up on a box and cut off all your hair and leave just a bob in front."

Left to right: Christy Ward, Patrick MacMahon, Willy Ryan (centre) Brigid MacMahon, Patrick Keane.

Photographer: Christy Greene.

Photographer: Christy Greene

HAVING A CHAT; GREENE'S HOTEL c. 1935

The three men standing in front of Greene's Hotel represent to an extent some of the characters living in Kinvara.

Pat Griffin (left) was a blacksmith, whose forge was located around the corner from the hotel. He married 'Cousineen' Keane at 40, and was the grandfather of John Griffin, the present owner of *The Ould Plaid Shawl* pub (the same building).

Pat Griffin and his brothers, Fergus and Tommy, were blacksmiths. They all spoke Irish, which would have stood them to good stead in their trade. Tommy, who worked in Galway, was nicknamed *lá garbh*, owing, no doubt, to his constant description of the weather when greeting people ('bad old day').

Griffin's forge was rented from the proprietor of Greene's Hotel, Thomas Greene (centre), described as a great 'character' who smoked *Woodbines* continuously and was not a man to mince his words. Also known as 'Pappy', children would greet him, and say: "Hello Pappy!"

Pappy Greene married the hotel's owner, Nora Lydon, in 1890. Her brother, Michael Fahy, of Fahy & Co, Galway (nicknamed 'Faheenco'), purchased the hotel and shop from a cousin, Thomas Fahy (father of the poet Francis Fahy). Michael then placed Nora and her first husband, Michael Lydon from Duras, in charge. She was soon widowed, however, when he died at 27 of TB, a prevalent disease at the time.

Pat Helebert (right) had a thriving hardware and grocery store on the quay, as well as an egg store nearby. He was the first to import bread into Kinvara from Limerick, collecting the hampers of loaves every evening at Ardrahan railway station. By this time, most of Kinvara's bakers had all but ceased baking bread.

Pat Helebert's loaves (grinders) were mentioned in a local poem about a wedding: "...Although we had an absence of chicken and cold ham, we had plenty of sweet bread, brown bread, Helebert's grinders and red jam..."

Photographer unknown
Courtesy of Paddy Greene

OLD WAYS AND CUSTOMS

The Connemara shawl covers all: It would have been quite common up to the 1940s or thereabouts to see the older women in the district wearing the traditional Connemara shawl, worn here, or the (black) Galway shawl. The lady in the centre came from near Clifden, Connemara, where she first met her future husband, Tommy Connolly (right), who worked for a time as a tea traveller in her area.

In his youth, Tommy 'Galyune', as he was called, was one of a group of local Kinvara lads selected by a leading tea company to promote their brand in the west of Ireland. The company's marketing technique involved Tommy and his companions calling on houses and leaving small sample packs of tea, wrapped in plain white paper, in the hope that householders would then become regular customers.

Older people in Kinvara also remembered a similar marketing ploy — finding tea on the kitchen table upon returning home. The roundsman would call again the following week expecting to collect his money.

Tom Connolly also collected the pennies and halfpennies at the chapel door, when church dues were being levied in this fashion. Being a native Irish speaker, he was also called upon to act as interpreter in local court cases. Paddy Connolly, the postman, was his son.

L-R: Jimmy Cunningham, Brigid Connolly (née King), Tommy Connolly. Location: possibly at Ardrahan railway station.

THE NEW CORN MILL c. 1941

The earliest method for grinding corn described in Kinvara folklore was the hand quern. The manually operated quern was round and made of stone. Having first dried the damp grains of corn (wheat, oats or barley) in front of the open fire at home, a quern was used for grinding sufficient flour for baking purposes.

Prior to the introduction of the paraffin-driven mills, Kinvara had one windmill, and three tidal mills located on the Doorus peninsula.

A new mill is delivered to the back of Greene's Hotel, where the proud owner, John Greene, has time to pose for the camera before unloading his prize new piece of equipment. On his right is his father, Thomas 'Pappy' Greene, who seems more interested, however, in getting on with the job.

The arrival of this machine heralded a boom time for John Greene, who would soon capture most of the grinding business in the town. Others using the smaller, paraffin oil driven *Lister* engine at the time included Winkle's on the square, Tommy Shaughnessey, and Paddy Halloran.

Aside of the barley, wheat and oats grown for home use or for sale, corn was also grown to feed one's livestock and for thatching purposes. From autumn on, when farmers' corn had been threshed, they would come to Greene's once a week or so, having first dried the grain at home. Up to four stone of wheat might be brought there at a time, or a 12-15 stone bag of barley for rolling (splitting the grain), for which Greene's had a separate machine.

Freshly-ground wheat made delicious bread, being ground either fine or coarse, and sometimes mixed with white flour to lighten it. Corn was rolled also for cattle and horses, or for sheep in the lambing season. It was then boiled and mixed with other foodstuffs.

The outbuildings in the background had fireplaces, which would suggest that they had been used as dwellings some time in the 1800s.

L-R: Mick Forde, Steven and Fergus Griffin, Thomas Keane, Oliver Ryan, John Greene, Thomas Greene, J.J. Conneely (behind), and Richie Burke.

Photographer unknown
Courtesy of Thomas Quinn

An activity often engaged in by husband and wife together, cutting weed at low tide was described as tiring, back-breaking work. In between tides, an unfinished, carefully-stacked heap had to be weighed down with rocks to prevent it from dispersing when the tide came in. The *climín*, carefully bundled together with ropes, then was floated ashore on the next tide.

A horse-cart could be loaded with approximately twice the amount of seaweed when it was dry, and it made a lighter load for the horse too. Vast quantities were transported each year to Loughrea, Ennis and beyond, where it was used mostly as fertiliser. Though considered to be of inferior quality, any seaweed washed ashore in storms would also be gathered, stacked and sold, or used at home. Such flotsam was known locally as *buaileadh isteach* (drift/blow-in).

Seaweed continues to be harvested on a smaller scale today, the seaweed now being collected by lorry for factories in Kilrush and Connemara. Used in the cosmetics industry and as a plant and animal food, it is still much-prized as an organic fertiliser by gardeners. An all but forgotten source of revenue today, one is reminded that in the year 1837 seaweed to the value of £20,000 was being brought ashore in Kinvara in Spring — an altogether staggering figure reported in Lewis's Topographical Dictionary. The photograph shows Tommy Quinn of Crushoa.

FLOATING THE CLEMEEN ASHORE
1940s

Seaweed was used widely as a fertiliser up to the 1950s. The *climín* — a raft of seaweed — is floated ashore with the aid of a pole. A clemeen was considered a 'good swimmer' or a 'bad swimmer', depending on the type of weed, and how it was constructed. Whether floated or brought ashore in a boat such as a *púcán*, seaweed harvesting, if not for private use, provided a welcome cash crop for anyone who was either leasing or in possession of 'shore rights'.

UNIDENTIFIED BOAT IN KINVARA HARBOUR 1930s

This photograph may have been prompted by a regatta or a festival of some kind, given the clothing of the boatmen, and the number of onlookers in the grounds of Seamount, or *Rinn na Mara*, as it was also called.

Boatmen from nearby Island Eddy came to Kinvara regularly on shopping expeditions but this *gleoiteóg* is not believed to have been from the island. Their boats, which they built themselves, did not contain a bowsprit, which is also missing at the front of this boat. More favoured than the *gleoiteóg* on Island Eddy was the smaller and more versatile *púcán*.

This view of Seamount House is much the same as it would have been in the mid-1800s, when its owner, Dr Denis J Hynes, was faced with an outbreak of typhus and cholera. Dr Hynes oversaw the building of the fine stone wall demarcating the shoreline, but did not live to see it completed.

Around the corner to the left of the boundary wall was the 'wicket', the original side-entrance to Seamount House. The new wall and gate section, erected at the behest of the Sisters of Mercy, is clearly visible.

Beside the slip is said to be the earliest part of the pier, built before French's time. The hut on the slip, known as Regan's shed, stands on the original site of a saw-pit. Logs of timber were cut into planks here up to the early 1900s by means of a pitsaw, a large saw operated by two men, one man standing above the pit and another below.

Ground water streaming out from a gap in the wall at this location provided one source of fresh water for nearby houses on the quay, before the installation of a mains water supply.

Photo: Cardall collection,
National Library, Dublin.

WALKING TO MASS, Main Street c. 1946

Thatched, tiled and slated roofs afford a tranquil, representative image of what might be any village street in Ireland in the mid 1940s. The neglected houses stand testimony to a period of declining prosperity and emigration that was to follow after the war.

This is one of the rare occasions when figures in an old postcard can be identified: Tommy Shaughnesssey, retired postman (right), ambles past the telegraph pole behind the youngster,

Martin Halvey, who is tearing along home. Ahead of them, outside Johnston's store, are John Ryan and Tom McCormack (centre right) on their way to 11 a.m. Mass.

The lady on the street opposite Jack Connell's house (foreground) is Nancy McInerney. They later married. She lived up the road, with her father, Tommy, who sold fish each week in Gort and Ennistymon. He travelled by horse and cart as far as Doolin or Galway to buy his fish.

1995

Photographer: John Greene
(with Capt O'Donoghue's
camera)

The young army captain had arrived from Germany with a friend and both men enjoyed a sing-song in Green's pub, nearby, where Sonny Green would play the accordion and sing a song or two. Apart from running the pub, he also bought turf-loads on the quay from Connemara boatmen on behalf of families in the neighbouring countryside. Their business done, the Connemara men would then have a few drinks in Sonny Green's pub and a sing-song would soon develop. Being more acquainted with jazz than with the traditional *sean nós* airs sung (in Irish) by the Connemara boatmen, the young American servicemen would later remark how all traditional songs sounded the same to their ears — sad and mournful.

VISITING G.I.; KINVARA QUAY
c. 1946

In the 1920s, May Leonard of Kinvara emigrated to the United States. On the ship she met her future husband, one Mikie O'Donoghue, from a neighbouring parish.

The Second World War has ended and May Leonard's son, Capt John O'Donoghue, is on leave from his army post in Germany. Her sister, Bridie, stands beside him; this was his very first visit to Ireland.

On the left, a man enters Pat Helebert's shop, which stocked mostly agricultural items. Regan's, with the donkey cart outside, sold hardware, tobacco and sweets. The blacksmith, Pat Griffin, lived in the end house and before that is Helebert's egg-store.

Market Day, Kinvara, Co. Galway.

TURF LORRIES ON MARKET DAY c. 1946

The war in Europe has ended, petrol is no longer being rationed, and the lorries are now in a position to re-capture the turf market. The brief upsurge in demand enjoyed by boatmen during the war years is now over.

Whereas a good hooker-load of turf would fill six separate horse carts, each in turn requiring the same process of loading and unloading as did the boats, the more efficient delivery of turf by road meant that fuel could now be delivered, in all weathers, right to your doorstep.

Before the arrival of lorries, deliveries from Flatley's coal-yard near the quay would have been made by horse and cart. Christy Corbett from Loughcurra townland was the first man to purchase a lorry for delivering turf to Kinvara. Turf lorries came to Kinvara on Wednesdays, and despite the presence of calves on the square, it is unlikely that the picture was taken at the Cattle Fair held on 28 February.

Traders bought turf from families such as the Smalls, Carters or Brennans from Connemara and Galway. Turf was sometimes bought on credit, the buyer paying the debt upon selling his cattle or sheep at the next fair.

Road transport more than anything else signalled the death knell of the maritime turf trade along the coast, though it would still take some years, as one man explained: "Boats came in every other day. I never saw the quay without boats. Then, in the early 1950s, I suppose it was, they couldn't compete with the lorries. There'd be lorry loads there on the market: All the bargaining, oh stop! The old people died away, and the young people didn't bother to cut the turf. Only the old people continued on cutting..."

THE LAST HOOKER c. 1956

The last hooker loaded with turf is said to have arrived in Kinvara in 1956. By that time, the maritime turf trade to the Kinvara coastline had all but ceased, with fuel now being collected and delivered by truck.

Some hookers such as *An Mhaighdean Mhara*, owned by Johnny Jimmy Mac Donncha of An Ceathrú Rua, Connemara, were still seen arriving in Kinvara in the early 1950s, mainly, it is believed, to visit relatives who had settled there.

A way of life slowly comes to end. The ending of the maritime turf trade resulted in the next generation having little use for their parents' boats. Many lay abandoned until the 1970s, when the revival of the sailing craft saw most of the surviving hookers re-fitted to sail in regattas around the country and abroad.

In their heyday, many social contacts developed and indeed some marriages took place between the boatmen and people living along the western coastline in places such as Ballyvaughan, Aughinish, New Quay, Parkmore, Kinvara, Tarea and Island Eddy. Boatmen like the McDonaghs, Grealishes, O'Sullivans, O'Briens and the Alans from Connemara were well-known.

A good hooker load of turf, costing £5-£6 around this time, filled six horse carts (or ten donkey carts). In the countryside, news arrived of boats sailing down the bay towards Parkmore and Kinvara quays. You called the neighbours, and they'd accompany you ('go Co') to lend a hand. Together with five or six carts you headed for the quay, and loaded the turf. Women and children later gathered and bagged the turf fragments, called 'cweerawns'

Photographer unknown
Courtesy of Úna Bermingham

(caoráin), with riddles being used to separate the bits of turf from the mold.

One man recalled the boats arriving in 1937: "I remember it clearly, 14 boats coming up the bay together, all in a line, gliding along the breeze." He continued: "There was terrible activity on the quay, with Sonny Greene buying a load for someone in the village or outside. They'd know to look at it if it was good stuff."

Photo: Cardall collection,
National Library, Dublin

KINVARA QUAY c. 1955

The panoramic view of the quay gives an idea of the enormity of effort to turn what had been a craggy shoreline into a fine, impressive harbour. Large limestone blocks used during the three major building phases of Kinvara pier and quay between 1773 and the early 1900s withstood all storms, gales and hurricanes. Yet it would take a mere 30 years or so in the fortunes of time and men to all but terminate its use as a port.

This tranquil scene of Kinvara quay in the mid 'Fifties is in stark contrast with the busy port in the early 1900s. Aside of John Joe Conneely's two small boats berthed at low tide by the quay wall, and Dr P.J. Greene's pleasure boat, the *Celtic* (centre), there is little to suggest that this was a thriving port a mere 50 years before.

The three-masted schooners are but a fading memory. Gone are the turf-laden hookers which loaded barley or timber and general provisions for their return journeys to Connemara.

Murphy's store stands tall and vacant-looking on the quay, though barley is still stored there. The trees on the left would soon make way for house-building purposes, as would the group of cottages on the right: known as the Claddagh (*claddach*: shore), most of those living on the Claddagh relied on fishing and boat-building for their livelihoods. By the 1980s the view would look quite different again.

Photo: Cardall collection,
National Library, Dublin

MAIN STREET 1956

Old and new: Michael John Corless's Ford Prefect IM 1422 stands parked outside his thatched premises, which for many years had served as a pub and grocery store. One of the last thatched houses on the street, it was destined to be knocked once the new corner building had been erected. Concrete blocks mark the site of the new house.

Seamount college, rising high above the other buildings in the background, proudly boasts its most recent extension, Marian House, a chapel and a science laboratory.

The *Vauxhall Wyvern* (left) belonging to building contractor, Michael John Bermingham, stands outside his home on the freshly-asphalted road, opposite Tom Gill's *Hillman*.

The corner shop beside the old water pump (right), which almost 100 years previously had housed the Temperance Hall, served as a hardware and grocery shop. It was occupied by Tom Gill who, by 1961, had the first TV in Kinvara. In the afternoons, there'd be 20 youngsters pressing in to watch *Bat Masterson*, the cowboy classic of its day.

Photo: D.T. Lucas, National Museum of Ireland, Dublin

PUBLIC WEIGHING SCALES 1951

Ass power and Shell power: A donkey stands in calm contemplation, as donkeys do, patiently awaiting its owner. Parked alongside is a Shell oil truck, an Austin, inanimately awaiting its driver. Both truck and ass are poles apart in terms of power, past and future, yet this is of little consequence to both drivers, who are possibly chatting over a pint in Winkle's Hotel.

The crane on the cobbled Market Square in Kinvara was still in use when this photo was taken in 1951. The scales, of course, were a great source of fun for children, who were constantly chased away for swinging on them.

Photo: D.T. Lucas, National Museum of Ireland, Dublin

THE CRANE AT WINKLE'S

The weighing scale, or crane, as it was better known, had many uses. Farmers going to sell their wool to buyers in Gort and elsewhere felt surer, having weighed their wool here first.

Corless's on the square bought wool from farmers as well. It was graded in an adjacent store, packed and then weighed. Wool buyers brought their own bagging material, and a day would be spent packing, with ropes and hooks being used to steady the immense packs. The wool was rolled and tightly packed in large square sheets of jute, whereupon it was sewn up, and weighed on the scales.

The crane was still in use in the early 1960s; bags of potatoes were weighed for customers such as the nuns in Seamount, who bought half a ton at a time. Quantities of corn, turnips and mangolds were also weighed, and the 4 stone, 2 stone and 1 stone weights seen here used as counterweights.

In later years, a weighbridge was located at the same spot, and used for weighing hay and suchlike. Carts were first weighed empty, and then when loaded. Sides were also fitted to the weighbridge, for the weighing of cattle.

OCTOBER SHEEP FAIR 1950s

By far the biggest fair of the year, the ram fair on 17 October saw buyers coming to Kinvara for rams and wethers, or the last breeding ewes of the season. The "earliest fair in Ireland" — a huge hogget fair — was held on 18 May, starting at 4 a.m. Yet another sheep fair took place on 15 Sept, while lambs and calves were sold in July. Farmers arrived a day or two before the fair to erect their pens, each time opting, if possible, to pick the same spot they had used the last time.

On this sunny autumn day, the town is crowded and money is changing hands. Sheep creels are heeled up against front doors right throughout the town, and out as far as the Castle Road. Children have a day off school, some helping out, minding stock, others — if they dare — badgering sellers for a 'fayrnin' *(féirín)*, a shilling or a sixpence. A flock of penned sheep stands tied together at the end of the row of houses, next to the entrance to Seamount convent, known as the 'wicket'.

Such fairs attracted hundreds of people from the hinterland. Buyers came from Loughrea and beyond to the October fair, having fattened and sold their ewes purchased in Kinvara in May. Hundreds of rams exchanged hands, and either were walked home or to the nearest railway station by hired drovers. It was not uncommon for 20-30 sheep to be left overnight in someone's field on their return trip. The practice of collecting tolls on such days would soon lapse, as fair days were replaced by the marts.

The hucksters would be there too, selling clothes and boots, reins for the horses or top coats. Along the quay, a house serves tea and bread with slices of mutton. Girls, employed for the day, enjoy the banter with the young men stepping in for a snack.

Persons identified: Man with stick in foreground: Matt Quinn (Moy); Patrick Curtin (Roo), far left, facing camera.

Photographer: Robert Cresswell

SELLING BONHAMS 1953

The Pig Fair was held on the first Monday of every month, except for July and August. Weaned piglets, or 'bonnifs' *(bainbh)*, could be purchased at the Square and fattened at home on farm produce and household scraps. They would be slaughtered sometime between October and March.

A big pig fair is said to have been held for many years on St Stephen's Day at Dunguaire, possibly dating back to late medieval times.

Minnie Halloran (foreground, wearing shawl) stands talking to her husband, Paddy, who had a small sawmill opposite the present Community Centre. Mrs Halloran kept a modest guesthouse, and reared pigs for the table.

When purchased, piglets could be brought home in the ever-so-handy bacon boxes of 'American Mate' (see page 39). Such boxes were also used at fairs, and filled with hay to keep the cattle still.

Prospective buyers inspect the contents of the ass cart, where piglets are huddled together beneath a canvas covering called a *bratach* or a *práiscín*.

The hay-littered square outside Winkle's Hotel bears testimony to a busy market day, judging from the carts, groups of onlookers and a huckster, better known locally as a *Seán Saor* (Bargain John), selling clothes from his van.

Times move on: Mary Keane, from the townland of Booleevin, has come prepared for rain. Between her umbrella, her bicycle, and the other two generations of public transport — the horse cart and the motor car — the picture captures something of the 1950s, when past was blending with present to forge the future.

Left to right: Paddy and Minnie Halloran (conversing, foreground) Jackeen Kelly, Crushoa, 3rd from Paddy wearing hat.

Jimmy Burke, Forge at Cartron townland.
Photographer: Robert Cresswell

MOUNTING A TIMBER HARROW 1950s

The common harrow was indispensable for preparing the land before ploughing, or indeed after sowing corn. Made of pitch pine and expertly joined by Christy Burke, a local carpenter, the harrow is now being worked by the blacksmith.

The implement has been pre-bored by the carpenter with an auger. Each hole is now prepared (squared) by driving one of the square harrow pins, red hot, into each hole, 24 in all. The blacksmith then reddens the 24 pins, pointing and squaring each one on the anvil.

The familiar clang clang of hammer on metal fills the forge as a group of men stand around discussing life's fortunes, and await their turn. The smith hammers away, ensuring the pins have a slight inward bend, and a barb to stop them falling out, once driven home.

Blacksmiths had plenty of work, supplying the farmer with spades, forks, iron bands for wheels, shoeing horses, etc.

Jimmy Burke, seen here, had two brothers, Jack and Christy, plying the same trade. Their father, John, a master farrier, served as a sergeant in the British army in the 1914-1918 war. Because of his training, he was put in charge of slaughtering horses. Apart from the Burkes, who in the early days had two fires and two bellows working in the forge, one could go to Pat Griffin or Paddy Connolly in the village.

SHOEING A WHEEL 1950s

Jack Burke, Forge at
Cartron townland.
Photographer:
Robert Cresswell

Having expanded the metal tyre on a brushwood fire nearby, the smith sets about cooling the tyre on a cartwheel. Steam hisses as Jack Burke, standing on the stock, cools the hot iron band mounted on the wooden wheel. Upon cooling, the iron will shrink and set tight around the cartwheel. The wheel will then be rolled to the nearest pool and submerged to swell the timber.

An iron stud steel band is also mounted on the stock of the wheel. The job of 'shrinking the iron' is completed on a round and flat purpose-made base of solid iron.

Carpenters and blacksmiths were largely dependent on each other's trades. Without the steel band, the timber wheel, however well made, will not last long on the rough country roads.

Another blacksmith, Pat Griffin, used to perform this same function during high tide at Kinvara quay, using an old circular piece of granite which was probably there long before his time.

DIGGING OR *'CRUBIN'* POTATOES
1950s

An average family would sow two acres of potatoes, providing an important food crop for the family and stock on the farm.

A copper sulphate mix (bluestone) had to be sprinkled in two stages over the developing haulms in summer to guard against the dreaded blight. Crop rotation was essential, and if seaweed — a common fertiliser at the time — was used for the potatoes this time, it would also do the barley crop to be planted there next year.

Every second drill was split with a horse-drawn plough, the coulter being raised or removed. Potatoes rooted or 'crubed' *(crúbadh)* from the centre drill were left in place, and the ones on either side thrown into that drill. This done, all odd drills were then ploughed, rooted and picked.

The men in the photo are wearing knee-caps made of sacking to cushion their knees during the arduous work. Women and girls doing the same work used aprons made from sacks of flour and known locally as 'prawshkeens' *(práiscíní)*.

By mid-afternoon, the men would be looking forward to their tea-break, or 'gurra' *(goradh)*. When completed, they will draw the gathered potatoes from the drills to a pit. Small potatoes are left behind, to be collected later for the pigs and hens.

Storage pits are then carefully constructed to protect the crop from rats and the elements. Orientated north-south where possible, the large pit resembles a turf-reek, but is smaller in size. The heap is first covered and insulated with a layer of thatch, which in turn is covered with a layer of clay.

When sowing potatoes in spring, children and women would follow behind the plough, removing stones and setting out the drills with seed, sliced potato pieces known as 'scillawns' *(sciolláin)*.

Left to right: Colie (Coilí) O'Loughlin and John Connolly.

Photographer: Robert Cresswell

Photographer: Robert Cresswell

SCALDING THE PIG
Connolly's farm, Gortaboy
Autumn, 1950s

A large family would slaughter two pigs a year, in October and March, and sell any surplus stock.

The two big ironware pots used during their lifetime to feed the pigs would now boil the large quantities of water (16 gals/72 ltrs.) necessary for the scalding operation. This facilitates the removal of hair by paring. The pig is dipped into the 3/4 barrel, first the front half, then the rear.

In the yard, recently-thatched stands of wheat and oats (left), are kept above ground to deter rodents. They will be threshed in spring; the barley has already been thrashed.

Pinpointing the location of a photo often revealed a marvellous memory for detail: "I can't understand that building... that definitely isn't me." "Oh it is," said Jimmy. "I'd know you five mile away."

"You couldn't ever remember that barrel could you? The house is putting me out.'Tis asbestos galvanised..." " There was no double barn in Ballycleara that time, I know that and you know it too. So it's not Pat..." Now, under your right thumb, that's...

Left to right: John and Miko Connolly; Mattie Connolly, the butcher and neighbour, and Michael Connolly.

Photographer unknown
Courtesy of Ann Niland

PARING THE PIG AT HYNES' YARD
Dunguaire townland 1950s

Neighbours and friends lend a hand. Before slaughtering, the pig's legs are tied to the front and rear shafts of an ass cart, the wheels sometimes being removed. The blood runs off the base of the cart and is collected in the galvanised bucket, to be used two days later in the making of delicious black pudding.

Next day, the pig is cut into portions and salted, weighted down and cured for 2-6 weeks in a barrel, then stored indoors. Prime cuts are divided amongst neighbours; the children who deliver these 'greeshkeens' (*gríscíní* — fillets of pork) will be given a shilling or two. The pig's head was also considered a delicacy, being first cut into four sections and boiled.

Local descriptions of such scenes were naturally quite vivid, but what was noticeable was that, in defining the *gender* of the pig, its sex depended entirely on that of the woman or man describing the scene: "Tie *him* to the shaft and stick him; it wouldn't take any length of time"..."Put *her* up on the table in the haggard and go paring away with the knives. And up again the next night, cut off the head first, four *crubes* (trotters), split down the middle, and salt..."

Left to right; foreground: Mattie Callanan, Anthony Staunton (sitting on barrel), Mike Hynes. Centre: Tom Connolly (holding pig) and Mattie Connolly (with glasses). Rear: Bridgie Winkle, and (..) Staunton.

MAGGIE SHAUGHNESSY
Schoolteacher c. 1962

At a time when schoolchildren often experienced the rigours of a disciplinary code at school, this image of the maternal, benevolent schoolteacher is what one likes best to remember. Maggie Shaughnessey was very well regarded by all who remembered her. She taught first in the Kinvara convent school, and later as an assistant in Killimoran National School in Gort. In her early years she cycled the many miles to her work, whatever the weather. From 1944-1958 she taught in the old national school, 10 km away in the townland of Corker, Kiltartan, which today serves as a heritage centre.

She was known to give the boys extra lessons in Maths and English, and always spoke in admiration of Lady Gregory.

Known to be "severe on the writing", she'd be constantly reminding young children to keep "above the line". In her day, 'staff rooms' and 'central heating' were concepts for the future. Former pupils remembered the chamber pot kept under her desk and the old primus stove on which she made tea for herself.

Maggie Shaughnessey lived at the back of her family's shop in the village, which sold delf and souvenirs such as egg-cups or plates with inscriptions like 'present from Kinvara'. An enterprising woman, in later years she also had a car for hire. Her next-door neighbour, John Connell, was the hackney driver, as was J.J. Conneely.

The Tully children, left to right: Frank, Ann, Patrick, and Mary. Dermot Cahill, next to teacher.

THATCHING; Main Street 1964

Depending on the quality of the material, a new coat of thatch could last 15 years and more. When harvested by mowing bar in the early 1900s, straw would be unbroken, and therefore of a much superior quality. Large scale usage of artificial fertilisers, together with the operation of combine harvesters in later years, produced a bigger grain but a thatching straw of much poorer quality.

Jack Connell (below ladder) occupied this house for a time — the third in a row of two-storey buildings, all of which were thatched. The middle house with the boarded windows stands derelict, and is not being re-thatched on this occasion; it may be patched in places. Paddy Joe Connolly's forge was situated at the entrance to the right.

Most of the thatching in the village was done by Martin Linnane, from the townland of Ballycleara. He is using wheaten straw, and putting 'combs' on the ridge. The evening sunlight shines down main street; soon it will be time for him to shake the straw from his bicycle and cycle home, or have a pint first in Tully's pub.

More than thirty years later, Martin Linnane, who was more accustomed to thatching the traditional, single-storey cottages, will be shown this photo, jogging his memory:

"Ah mother of God, all gone... look at the thatch, all gone, never to be seen again... And it's me thatchin'! On my oath, I was above in it. That's a while ago... Wasn't it a high house to go up on. We were young then, we didn't give a damn!"

Photographer: Enda Muldoon

1995

Merriman Inn & Restaurant, opened 18-04-'97.

MOUNTAIN VIEW HOTEL
Kinvara 1964

The Merriman Inn (below, left) opened its doors in April 1997, on the former site of the Mountain View Hotel, which opened around 1939 and closed 30 years later.

Its proximity to the Burren made the Mountain View hotel a popular choice for botanists from Trinity College in Dublin, as well as speleologists. Groups of fishermen came in the summer and fowlers at Christmas. Cyclists touring the countryside also stayed there, as did the casts of travelling shows coming to town, and a number of teachers who taught in Seamount college.

Better known as John Peter O'Grady's, the thatched hotel (right) was formerly used as a bakery run by his father, Martin O'Grady, a Kilfenora baker who came to work for the Corless's on the square in the early 1900s. Both father and son initially had an egg-grading store at the side of the building, and sold poultry and rabbits also. In the 1950s a room was leased to a hairdresser, Kitty Duffy from Gort.

John Peter also had an ice-cream parlour, and reputedly was the first man to sell ice-cream in Kinvara. On their way to Trácht beach on a Sunday, people stopped to buy a wafer or a threepenny cone, topped with a delectable drop of cordial. Children smacked their lips at the delicious little buns and pastries or wedding cakes, made by him and displayed on crispy white doilies on cake stands in the window.

Amongst the hotel's residents who later became famous were the actors, Cyril Cusack, Sheila Richards, and Joan Greenwood. Other maestros of the stage included Micheál Mac Liamóir and Anew McMaster who would stay a week when cycling around the Burren. The shed loft pictured to the right of Winkle's shop is where J.P. O'Grady kept the hay for his stock; the cows around the back were milked each day by Mrs O'Grady herself.

Photographer:
Enda Muldoon

Mikey Traynor plied the cobbler's trade in his little shop next door to Winkle's (left) up to about the time this photograph was taken. Afterwards the same building was used at different stages as a butcher's shop by Gerry and Marty Fallon, prior to the construction of Fallon's supermarket, opposite, in 1989.

Winkle's grocery shop was run by Katie and later, by her sister, Chrissie Winkle.

The hotel has a relatively new coat of thatch, explained the thatcher himself, an old man when shown this photo in 1996: "Oh, that's O Grady's house, I know it. I thatched it twice. 'Twasn't long done! That's probably John Peter sitting on the seat.. Jesus wasn't it grand too.. The last time I did it — the two sides — was when Hurricane Debbie blew it off in 1961..."

AERIAL VIEW, KINVARA VILLAGE 1950s

This bird's-eye view of Kinvara in the 1950s shows at a glance how little of the town's general infrastructure has changed during the previous 50 years.

Today's aerial view would look quite different, with more land reclaimed, less (though more intensive) agriculture, and many bright new bungalows unconnected with the farming landscape.

In the picture we see a quiet harbour, with no boat in sight. Opposite Regan's shop (left) on the quay, two cart-loads of seaweed await collection by a farmer, who will pay for them when he sells his sheep. Behind Regan's is the old church of saint Coman, of which the gable is still visible amongst the trees.

On the very right of the picture lies the shoreline known as the Claddagh *(claddach),* and behind the row of three houses is the hilly location known as the *Cruachán,* or *Cnocán na mBád,* a popular place for children playing amongst the hills and valleys. It was at *Cnocán na mBád* that master boat-builders like the Keanes and Patsey Brannelly built great hookers such as the *Lord,* and *An Tonaí.* To launch the boats, they would make a ramp several feet high of seaweed and pull the boat down to the shoreline over the seaweed.

In the background we can see the Burren uplands, with Slievecaran on the right. At the foot of this mountain are the ruins of St Coleman Mac Duach's chapel and the saint's hermitage.

It is a sunny day in August, and in the fields, the haystacks are clearly visible — 'trammed' but not saved. Large areas of tilled land and pasture (right) mark the original scrublands cleared for agriculture.

Soon will come the 1960s and the subsequent transformation of rural communities throughout Ireland. As Kinvara says goodbye to the 1950s, the countryside braces itself for change.

A new sense of identity and pride of place becomes all the more significant.

Photographer unknown
Courtesy of Paddy Greene

Tír Eolas is a publishing firm based in Doorus, Kinvara, Co. Galway.

Since it was established in 1985, **Tír Eolas** has published six Guides and Maps, covering the Burren, South Galway, Kinvara and Medieval Galway.

Tír Eolas Books

The Book of the Burren, edited by Jeff O'Connell and Anne Korff, 1991. A Natural History and Human History of the famous West of Ireland Burren.
ISBN   1-873821-00-X PB.   Price   £11.95
            1-873821-05-0 HB.   Price   £15.95

The Shannon Floodlands, by Stephen Heery, 1993. A Natural History of the Shannon Callows.
ISBN   1-873821-02-6 PB.   Price   £9.95

Not a Word of a Lie, by Bridie Quinn-Conroy, 1993. A portrait of "growing up" in the West of Ireland.
ISBN   1-873921-01-8 PB.   Price   £6.95

The Book of Aran, edited by John Waddell, J.W. O'Connell and Anne Korff, 1994. A Natural History and Human History of the Aran Islands, Co. Galway.
ISBN   1-873821-03-4 PB.   Price   £15.95
            1-873821-04-2 HB.   Price   £25.00

Women of Ireland, by Kit and Cyril Ó Céirín, 1996. A biographic dictionary of Irish women from earliest times to the present.
ISBN   1-873821-06-9 PB.   Price   £9.95